Effective Use of Volunteers in Hospitals, Homes and Agencies

Effective Use of Volunteers in Hospitals, Homes and Agencies

By

HAROLD P. KURTZ

Director of Public Relations
Lutheran General Hospital
Park Ridge, Illinois

and

MARGARET BURROWS

Director of Volunteer Services
Lutheran General Hospital
Park Ridge, Illinois

CHARLES C THOMAS · PUBLISHER
Springfield · Illinois · U.S.A.

Published and Distributed Throughout the World by
CHARLES C THOMAS • PUBLISHER

BANNERSTONE HOUSE
301-327 East Lawrence Avenue, Springfield, Illinois, U.S.A.
NATCHEZ PLANTATION HOUSE
735 North Atlantic Boulevard, Fort Lauderdale, Florida, U.S.A.

With THOMAS BOOKS *careful attention is given to all details of
manufacturing and design. It is the Publisher's desire to present books
that are satisfactory as to their physical qualities and artistic possibilities
and appropriate for their particular use.* THOMAS BOOKS *will be true
to those laws of quality that assure a good name and good will.*

Printed in the United States of America
W-2

To the volunteers of Lutheran General Hospital

ACKNOWLEDGMENTS

IN WRITING THIS BOOK, the authors are indebted to many people, groups and organizations for their aid, encouragement and cooperation . . . to the administrative staff of Lutheran General Hospital; to the many volunteer directors; to our friends and colleagues at Lutheran General: Ted Jacobsen, John Kaufmann, Fredric Norstad, Paul Johnson, Dean Kruckeberg, Jeannette Rosenbrook, Evelyn Parks, Zinia Straus and Jim Wylie.

We are also indebted to Ernest Tisil for his aid in providing illustrations; to our secretaries, Ruth Berg and Ruth Johnson; to all of the Service League members, and finally, to our respective spouses, Bus and Grace, for their help and understanding during the writing of this book.

CONTENTS

Effective Use of Volunteers in Hospitals, Homes and Agencies

Chapter I

THE VOLUNTEER PROGRAM

Aмerica is a nation of volunteers. A recent study by the United States Department of Labor states that there are twenty-two million Americans giving volunteer service in one form or another. That means some 16 percent of all Americans fourteen years and older are giving volunteer service. The same study indicates that by 1980, the estimated worth of volunteer service would be thirty billion dollars. It is probably incorrect to classify volunteers as an "industry." Yet, any effort which employs the services of twenty-two million people in the multibillion-dollar category can certainly be classified as a major industry.

We do not want to imply that the subject of volunteers in this book is going to be viewed as a crassly commercialized subject, on an economic par with the automotive industry, agriculture or steel production. Rather, these figures are cited to show that volunteers play a big role in American life and that the volunteer must be taken seriously.

The volunteer is the greatest untapped resource available to hospitals, agencies and institutions. Failure to utilize the volunteer effectively is as much of a crime for a hospital as it would be for a hospital to knowingly fail to provide the latest life-saving drugs in its pharmacy.

A BIT OF HISTORY

Consider the roles volunteers play in our nation today and those which they have played in the past. The patriots of the Continental Congress were volunteers. They gathered as a volunteer group with no thought of compensation. The Minute Men of Concord and Lexington were volunteers.

As new states came into the Union one by one, their constitutional assemblies were manned by volunteers. On the local level in pioneer days, roads were built and schools were opened by volunteers.

Today, the volunteer is an essential part of the American governmental system. It is true that there are many salaried governmental officials. But for every salaried official there are scores of unsalaried officials or those serving at salaries so low that for all practical purposes they are volunteers. School boards, volunteer firemen, Civil Defense units, municipal zoning boards, library boards, planning commissions, civic advisory groups and a multitude of others are all volunteers—receiving little or no compensation.

As is the case with many other honors, the honor of being the first American hospital volunteer probably belongs to that leading citizen of Philadelphia, Benjamin Franklin. It was Franklin who in 1751 organized the first hospital in the nation.

The Civil War saw probably the first major large-scale volunteer efforts on the part of American citizens caring for the sick and wounded. One very important volunteer was Cordelia Harvey out of whose efforts came the Veterans Administration Hospitals. Walt Whitman served in Washington hospitals.

The end of the Civil War saw an increase in the number of hospitals opened in the country, many of them started by groups of volunteers. These volunteers continued to serve after the hospitals were opened, but they often continued their interest through fund-raising support—the traditional hospital auxiliary.

A great deal has been written and said about the Judeo-Christian tradition in volunteering and this, too, forms part of the history of volunteering. It is from this historical background that the role of the modern volunteer has emerged. There is good historical precedent for a hospital volunteer program. But historical precedent is not a good enough reason.

On the hospital scene, the entire hospital system in the United States is usually described as a "voluntary hospital system." Each hospital is independent, originated by volunteers who have seen the need for a hospital.

These hospitals in turn are governed by trustees who are

volunteers who serve without compensation. Volunteerism is a way of life in America.

THE REASONS FOR A VOLUNTEER PROGRAM

Those who have operated hospitals successfully for many years without volunteer help may ask, Why should the hospital have a volunteer program? To the administrators of hospitals with ongoing volunteer programs, the answer is obvious. There are many reasons why a hospital should establish a volunteer program:

First, volunteer service enhances the quality of care given to patients. There are more hands available to do the multitude of jobs which must be done in the hospital. Perhaps the volunteer only arranges the flowers in the vase for the patient. Nonetheless, this is important to the patient, and it would have to be done by someone. Thus the volunteer frees the nurse's hands for a more important task.

Second, volunteers help prevent depersonalization. As hospitals become larger, there is always a possibility of the depersonalizing influence setting in. The effective use of volunteers can be very beneficial in maintaining the personal touch.

Third, volunteers provide complementary skills. The volunteer can be more than just an extra person to run errands and deliver flowers.

Fourth, a good volunteer program meets the needs of the volunteers themselves.

Let us look at these points in greater detail.

Enhancing Quality of Care

When volunteers are available, there are more hands to perform the multitude of jobs which must be done in the hospital. The volunteer can be an effective supplement to the existing work force of an institution.

Combatting Depersonalization

As hospitals grow larger and more specialized, depersonalizing influences may become apparent. The effective use of volunteers can be of great assistance in maintaining the personal touch.

A good volunteer program can act as a bridge between the professional and the patient. A volunteer can afford to spend more time with a patient—time which can not be spent by a highly skilled professional. A volunteer can also spend the time in institutions which have pressing shortages of skilled personnel such as nurses.

One study indicates that a major problem facing hospitals is this depersonalization or dehumanizing element. Scientific objectivity has been stressed, often at the expense of the human element.

A good volunteer program can help a hospital retain warmth, personality and humanization.

Community Responsibility

Most hospitals are community hospitals—that is, they are operated for the benefit of all segments of the community on a not-for-profit basis. Just as a community hospital has a responsibility to provide for the health needs, so, too, it has a responsibility to provide an outlet for men and women interested in providing volunteer service.

Providing Complementary Skills

The volunteer is no longer merely an extra pair of hands to perform exclusively routine menial chores. The volunteer is capable of performing many tasks within the hospital or institution.

A major, albeit quiet revolution has taken place in hospitals during the past generation. Registered nurses today are carrying out professional duties once reserved for the physician. The licensed practical nurse is performing the duties once the domain of the registered nurse. The aide is taking over many of the jobs formerly handled by the LPN. So it goes.

The United States Department of Labor survey points out that the higher a person's educational background, the more likely this person is to volunteer. As a result, volunteers possess a vast reservoir of talent. But a reservoir does little good just sitting there. It must be tapped to be useful.

An inventory of available volunteer skills must be made and

efforts made to put these skills to use. Training and orientation are needed.

Meeting Needs of Volunteers

There exist within many people the desire and need to volunteer of their time and talents. Other chapters will discuss this in more detail, but there is a definite need for people to volunteer—not for all people, but for a sizable segment. It is up to the hospital to meet this need.

It is not stating the case too strongly to say that a hospital which does not provide an opportunity for significant volunteer service is not completely fulfilling its responsibility to the community.

Other Aspects

Among the more than 7,000 hospitals in the United States, only about half report an organized volunteer program. Undoubtedly the percentage is much lower for homes, agencies and other institutions.

As noted earlier in this chapter, one out of every eight Americans over the age of fourteen years is providing some volunteer service. This is impressive until one reverses the figures and points out that seven out of every eight Americans over the age of fourteen do not volunteer in any manner.

Obviously, no one would ever see a time when this figure would hit 100 percent. Yet, even if the figure could be doubled, this would provide the nation's hospitals, homes, schools, agencies and institutions with an utterly unbelievable amount of time, talent and ability to provide for the betterment of the nation.

It is important that those responsible for the hospitals, homes and other agencies recognize the importance and significance of volunteers. The question they should ask is not, "Why a volunteer program?" but "Why not a volunteer program?"

A good volunteer program, like any other program, demands leadership, support and the desire for excellence. Not every hospital can or should be a giant medical center. Not every volunteer program can provide a complete range of volunteer services. If an institution is meeting a definite need, it can help meet this need by a more effective utilization of volunteers.

WHAT THIS BOOK IS

This book is written to discuss the effective utilization of volunteers. Since the authors are hospital people, most of the discussion and examples will speak of hospitals. However, in almost all cases, the word "hospital" can be used interchangeably with home, agency, school or other institution.

The primary emphasis is on volunteers in the health field, but again this can be broadened to cover social service agencies and others.

It is the hope of the authors that this chapter and the succeeding chapters will help provide the stimulus for more effective volunteer programs in the nation.

WHAT THIS BOOK IS NOT

This book is not intended as a technical reference. It does not go into great details on many of the technical aspects of setting up and running a volunteer program. For this type of information, there are several volumes available and they are listed in the bibliography section of this book.

Chapter II

WHY PEOPLE VOLUNTEER

IF A HOSPITAL or agency is to have a successful volunteer program, it is essential that those responsible for the program take into account some of the reasons why people volunteer. It would be nice if this chapter could list a given number of basic factors which motivate all people to volunteer. It is not that simple; the reasons are complex and vary from person to person.

This chapter will attempt to provide some of the needed understanding about the factors which motivate people to volunteer. Keep in mind that it is not essential to understand the motivation of each individual volunteer. Rather it is important to know what motivates people in general to volunteer. If one understands these motivations, then a volunteer program can be established which meets the basic needs which cause a person to volunteer. As a result, it will be easier to obtain and retain volunteers.

BASIC MOTIVATIONS

Psychologists have established that all people have certain basic needs which create the motivation for various activities.

The psychologist A. H. Maslow lists these five factors as the basic needs of the human:

1. The bodily processes.
2. The need for safety.
3. Love.
4. Status and the acceptance by the group.
5. General adequacy, creativity and self-expression.

There is no need to discuss the first two points. However, the latter three points certainly play a part in the understanding of the motivation of volunteers. Let us discuss them in greater detail.

Love

Every person has the need for love—to love and to be loved. It would be nice to think that every volunteer is motivated to serve entirely by love for her fellow human beings. It is true that this love is a factor which motivates people to volunteer. Yet, from a realistic point of view, the need to love is not the only factor. The need to be loved enters in this context as well. A person who has not received love in a family setting, or who may be alone in the world can find this need met by volunteering in a setting where she can receive a feeling of love for the work she does. The motivation to be loved can often be a greater force in motivating volunteers than the need to love.

The Bible states that love is the greatest blessing in the world. It can be the greatest force in the motivation of volunteers. A successful program must take this into account—the need to love and the need to be loved.

Status and Acceptance by Group

Group acceptance and status were once major motives for volunteer work. A person volunteered because it was the accepted thing to do by certain segments of society. The social leader volunteered in the tradition of *noblesse oblige*: those who wanted to be social leaders volunteered so they could be considered in the same category.

This tradition remains very much alive today. Certain hospital and social-service volunteer groups in the country can count in their memberships the best-known family names in America. There is no question that serving as a volunteer in certain causes and certain institutions does give status to the individual doing it.

Of course, not all motivation in this category comes from high society. The acceptance by the group or peers is also a common motivating factor. Many teen-age volunteers originally began to serve because of a need to belong to the group. It's the thing to do.

A great deal of the acceptance of the Peace Corps, VISTA

and similar programs has undoubtedly been brought about by this need for group acceptance.

This is not to belittle those who serve. The important thing to remember is *that* people serve not *why* they serve.

If volunteering helps meet these basic needs in the individual then the volunteer program is having a far-greater effect than a program which just provides a certain amount of service. A gift, after all, should provide joy not only to the recipient but to the giver as well. The same holds true for a volunteer program.

General Adequacy, Creativity and Self-Expression

This is an increasingly impersonal age. People are becoming more and more dependent upon others in their work and lives. There is less and less opportunity for people to demonstrate creativity in their jobs. As a result, people who lack opportunity in their jobs compensate in other ways. A person can write a novel in the evening hours; he can climb mountains on weekends or can camp on his vacation. All of these help meet these basic needs.

A person can also volunteer his services or talents and help meet these needs which he is not receiving on his job. A good volunteer program will provide opportunity to express creativity, to demonstrate adequacy and to show self-expression. A good volunteer program can help a person meet these needs.

In turn, the good volunteer program director recognizes that this is what many people are searching for when they volunteer. If they are to meet these needs, then programs must change or be set up to meet these basic needs.

Mrs. Charles Balfanz, a long-time leader in hospital volunteer work, calls for a "renaissance" in attitudes to bring about this change. Writing in the *Volunteer Leader,* she points out that volunteers in hospitals (and other agencies as well) are changing from supplementary to complementary jobs. She says a "new breed" of volunteer is emerging. To this "new breed" of volunteer, the altruistic motive of helping others may be less important than the desire for self-development and self-expression. As a result, these volunteers want jobs which offer challenge and are demanding.

If there is a "renaissance" now occurring in volunteerism (and the authors share Mrs. Balfanz's views), then those responsible for volunteer programs must recognize that these creativity and self-expression needs are basic factors in the development of the program.

The volunteer is asking to be taken seriously. If the volunteer is taken seriously, the hospital will be richer for it. If the volunteer is not taken seriously, then she will seek another avenue for her service and the hospital will be poorer for it. The volunteer program which fails to consider these factors on motivation will find that its program is not meeting the fullest potential.

It would be possible to write chapter after chapter on the factors which motivate people. However, the purpose of this book is not to examine in detail these motivational factors, but to sketch them out and show how they relate to the modern volunteer program. An understanding of the basic motivations will help make a more worthwhile program.

Dr. Alan N. Schoonmaker of the Carnegie-Mellon University of Pittsburgh, Pennsylvania, has made a study of these as they relate to the voluntary organizations and reported the findings in the *Public Relations Journal.*

> Applied psychological principles and actions rule rather than force or economic rewards are the chief methods of motivating people to contribute both time and money to volunteer and charitable organizations.
> Although these principles have been verified in countless investigations, a few people always object to them. They feel that they emphasize the base side of man and ignore his nobility. They prefer a picture of man which is more noble, which emphasizes what he should be rather than what he is.

As Dr. Schoonmaker points out, volunteer organizations work with people—as they are, not necessarily as they should be. He lists several principles in understanding the motivation of volunteers.

Principle One

People act to satisfy their own needs and desires, not the needs of the organization or other people.

It is fine to recruit volunteers by telling them how much good they will be doing for others. Yet, they will respond because by doing good for others they are meeting the needs within themselves. By responding to this call, the volunteer gains this feeling of inner satisfaction. Or, by volunteering he may also be relieving a feeling of guilt.

An organization may have many needs. Yet an appeal based solely on these needs will fail. The appeal has to touch the potential volunteer by providing for his own needs and desires.

Based on this premise then, to motivate a potential volunteer, it is necessary to emphasize the benefits and satisfaction which will be gained to himself personally, not the benefits which will accrue to the organization or the people it serves.

This may sound a bit calculating and cold-blooded. Yet, it remains a fact of life in motivating people. The volunteer organization which ignores this aspect of motivation will be less than successful.

Of course, this doesn't mean that a volunteer organization must be set up in a blatantly cold-blooded fashion.

Principle Two

"People behave to satisfy their real motives not the motives they should have."

Dr. Schoonmaker gives as an example the anti-smoking campaign waged by numerous health groups. Health agencies expend a great deal of energy attempting to get people to stop smoking. It is an unusual smoker who will not agree that smoking is bad and that he should quit. Yet, despite anti-smoking campaigns, he still continues to smoke. Why? By smoking he is satisfying a real craving on his part.

Carry this over to the volunteer concept. Every person will admit that he could be a hospital volunteer, that he is needed and that he could make a significant contribution by so doing—yet he does not volunteer.

Why? Because basically he does not *want* to do it, no matter how much someone else thinks he should do so. Unless an appeal can be made to his other motives, a person will not volunteer simply because he should do so.

With this principle in mind, the volunteer organization

should attempt to find out what will motivate potential volunteers and then proceed to concentrate on these real motives, rather than dwelling on what should be the motivation of the people.

Principle Three

"People have many different motives. Most of their behavior is caused by a combination of these motives."

This gets back to what was discussed earlier in the chapter. In discussing the basic motivations or drives of people, it was pointed out not only love, but the need for status and acceptance by the group and the need for creativity and self-expression play a major role in the forces shaping a person's life.

Different people are motivated by many different aspects of these basic drives. To successfully motivate people generally requires a shotgun approach to hit many of these factors which motivate people.

It should be understood that these principles represent one man's ideas on the motivation of volunteers. Others who have studied this field, however, reach similar conclusions.

True, there is tendency on the part of the professionals in volunteer work to emphasize the work of the hospital or agency, the love of mankind or the sense of service. It would be wrong to say that these are not factors in influencing people to volunteer their efforts.

One cardinal point to keep in mind: in motivating a person to volunteer or in motivating a person who has volunteered, remember that the volunteer is a person, a human being. The donning of the cherry pink uniform of a hospital volunteer does not change that person.

That person responds as any other human being would respond. There is no such thing as a "volunteer personality" which demands a specialized approach or procedure.

Keeping People Motivated

It is not enough merely to interest a person in volunteering. Once a person has offered his services, it doesn't mean he'll stay active and interested.

Motivation applies not only to getting a person to volunteer in the first place, it applies equally to keeping a person well motivated in the work being done.

Future chapters in this book discuss the basic concepts in providing recognition for volunteers, for providing additional training, and for providing expanded opportunity.

All of these and others are part of the motivational aspects of the volunteer program. All of these points should be considered by the hospital trustees, administrator and volunteer director when planning a full-scale volunteer program.

This does not mean that any of these people have to have a graduate degree in psychology to have a successful program. It does require, however, a basic understanding of the motivational aspects of the human being.

The U. S. Department of Labor in its study *Americans Volunteer* surveyed volunteers and found some 200 reasons why people said they volunteered. The most common reasons given by people for volunteering were the following:

1. *A sense of duty.* They saw that work had to be done and felt obliged to help do it. Or, they did it because they believed in the organization doing the work. Or, because of membership in a particular organization, they felt they should do the work.

2. *A desire to help people.*

3. *A liking to do the work.* Volunteers enjoyed the work, they had an interest in the work or the organization doing the work.

4. *They were asked to do the work.* A friend, relative or another person asked them to help.

It is interesting to note that a University of Michigan study found a correlation of people who volunteer and the number of appliances owned by the volunteer's family. The greater the number of appliances the more likely a member of the family is apt to be an active volunteer. (Perhaps recruitment efforts are misdirected. Maybe a good recruitment campaign should hire the local appliance service man as a consultant to find out which families in town have the most appliances and thus are the most likely candidates for volunteering.)

SUMMARY

There have been countless books written on the subject of motivation. Not everything can be covered in these short pages.

Basically, the successful volunteer director today must have a working knowledge of these two functions of motivational psychology:

1. How to motivate people to get them to volunteer.

2. Once they have volunteered, they must be motivated to continue their interest in volunteering.

A program which can provide these two points will be a successful volunteer program.

Chapter III

THE VOLUNTEER TODAY

IN THE HOSPITAL and health field, the volunteer represents one of the major untapped resources. No other single hospital service has developed as rapidly as volunteers, and no other hospital group has such great potential for recruitment.

Although volunteers are readily available at most hospitals and other health agencies, volunteers can have only the potential which the hospital provides. A volunteer is useful for a hospital only if she is an effective volunteer who has a meaningful task to perform.

A volunteer, although unpaid in dollars, still requires an investment on the part of the hospital. Only if a hospital is willing to make an investment in volunteers will they provide a return to the hospital.

There are many excellent volunteer programs in American hospitals. There is no good reason why almost every hospital in the nation cannot have an effective volunteer program providing service to patients, families and community.

But an effective volunteer program will not happen by itself. Just as it takes hard work, resources, dedication and constant training to develop a good staff of hospital employees, so must the hospital constantly seek to recruit, develop and train good volunteers.

A hospital volunteer program, like any other aspect of the hospital operation, can be only as good as there is a desire for excellence on the part of the trustees and administration of the hospital. Good volunteer programs do not just happen any more than good hospitals just happen. They must be planned, guided, nurtured and constantly evaluated and reevaluated.

Once upon a time volunteers in the hospital ranked about

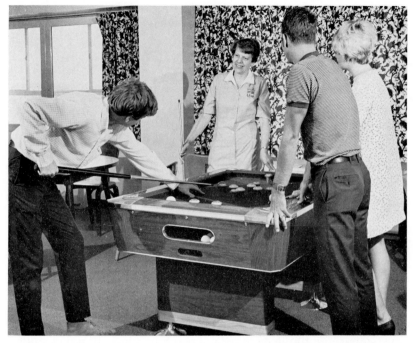

FIGURE 1.   A game of bumper pool can be useful therapy for teenagers on a psychiatric floor of a hospital. Volunteers can be highly useful in situations such as these.

on a par with the parsley on the roast beef. They were nice to have around, they added a little something extra to the hospital, they looked nice, but no one really thought they did much.

Today—fortunately—this is all changing. No longer is the volunteer relegated to being a member of the auxiliary. In the best hospitals the volunteer is recognized as a vital member of the hospital team. Giving of her time and talents, she not only serves the hospital and its patients, but she also acts as an invaluable liaison between the hospital and the community.

The volunteer is no longer a society matron with a little extra time on her hands, seeking to do the socially acceptable job of volunteering to help the less fortunate members of society. Gone is this condescension.

The modern volunteer may be male or female, young or old.

The modern volunteer may be a busy career woman who gives up a night or two a week of her valuable time. She may be a community leader who feels she has time for something besides the country club. The modern volunteer may be a retired business executive, a lonely widow, an off-duty fireman, a teen-age boy or girl or come from a variety of backgrounds.

Just as hospitals are constantly changing, so must volunteer programs change to keep pace with hospital progress.

In a recent year, 4,557 hospitals reported some 600,000 volunteers giving over thirty-two million hours of service. Ten years ago these figures were one-third this size.

A decade ago, only a scattering of hospitals had a salaried director of volunteer services. Today hundreds of hospitals have salaried directors whose prime responsibility is organizing, directing and training volunteers.

Every wage-earning employee of a hospital needs training, guidance and orientation for his position. No hospital would say to a newly hired nurse, "There are the patients—go to work." No hospital would hire a housekeeping aide and expect her to find her cleaning supplies on her own and decide where to work and how to go about her cleaning duties.

Obviously it just does not make good sense to do this. If it does not make good sense for a hospital to treat its employees this way, it does not make good sense to expect its volunteers to function in this manner.

BOARD PHILOSOPHY

A good volunteer program starts right at the top with the board of trustees of the hospital. Of all people connected with the hospital, the trustees should be the most attuned to volunteer service, for they themselves are volunteers.

True, perhaps they do not wear a distinctive uniform or receive a pin for a thousand hours of service. But just like the teen-age candy-striper, the trustee is volunteering his time and services for the hospital and the community which it serves.

The governing board of the hospital should adopt as a statement of policy its regard for hospital volunteers. The board should have the final voice on volunteer matters just as it has the final voice on medical staff and hospital policies. The trustees should establish a means of receiving regular reports from the volunteer organization, either through ex officio board membership or through a periodic attendance at trustees meeting by the volunteer president, director or designated representative.

Without strong support of the board of trustees, no volunteer program can be effective. The board should set guidelines and policy. It should allow the volunteer to function freely but should still exercise effective control of the program.

The board should budget for volunteer services just as it budgets for laboratory, administration, nursing service and all hospital departments. There is a temptation to have the auxiliary fund raising effort pay for the cost of a volunteer director and related expenses, but this should be avoided.

ROLE OF ADMINISTRATION

It is the role of the hospital administration to carry out the policy of the board on volunteers. It is up to the administrator to seek out and hire any other department head.

The hospital administration could provide guidance and direction for the volunteer program in the same manner as it oversees other departments. It should not seek to run the volunteer program any more than it would seek to run a cytology laboratory.

A good hospital administrator will seek out and hire a competent director of volunteers, see that the director is following board and hospital policy and allow the director to do her job. The director of volunteers should be on a par with other professional departments.

The volunteer director should report to the hospital administrator, not to an auxiliary board. The volunteer director should work for the hospital, not for the volunteer group.

HOW HOSPITALS ARE CHANGING

The modern hospital is no longer isolated from the community which it serves. It is a vital part of the community, not only standing ready to serve the sick and the injured, but serving many parts of the total community.

As this concept grows, the hospital becomes more and more active and involved in becoming a leader for the betterment of the total health problems of the community. Through its changing relationship with the community, the hospital is becoming more and more involved in the total life of the community.

With the changing role of the hospital, also comes a changing concept regarding volunteers. The volunteer is in a unique position of being something of a "bridge" or a transition between the hospital and its community.

The volunteer can help interpret to the community the changing role of the hospital, and the volunteer can also bring to the hospital the needs and feelings of the community, thus developing a two-way communication.

The Reverend Fredric M. Norstad, D.D., a pioneer in pastoral

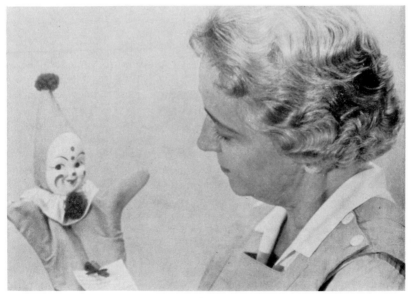

FIGURE 2. Many a child's stay in the hospital has been lightened by a puppet made and presented to the youngster by hospital volunteers. This is typical of the many things which volunteers do to help make hospitalization less traumatic for patients.

clinical training and philosopher of hospitals gave this profile of the modern volunteer:

A volunteer is concerned. Her concern finds its deepest dimension in an identification with those she serves. They are not objects, but rather brothers and sisters in the family of God and in the family of man.

A volunteer is creative. Her concern always results in creativity. Concern becomes the necessity that mothers inventiveness and creativity. It seeks for many and more profound ways of communicating an eloquent 'I Love You'!

A volunteer is excited. She is involved in the most exciting endeavor of which mankind is capable—meaningful relationship with others. To be "involved in mankind" is always man's most significant effort.

A volunteer is flexible. This is another way of saying that she is not selfish. She works not to satisfy her own ego needs, but joins her efforts with those of others for the good of the people she serves. In doing so she sees the offering of herself not individualistic but in corporate terms. In any team endeavor, flexibility is a key requirement.

A volunteer is loyal. She puts the needs of others and the organization in which she serves ahead of her own personal interests or wishes. She protects the patient from gossip—even her own, and she reflects in positive terms the best efforts of the organization.

A volunter is 'professional.' This may seem like a contradiction in terms. I simply mean that she sets the highest standard for her offering and conducts herself in a manner which reflects her dedication and reveals the high value which she attaches to her service— always striving to improve the skills with which she does her work.

A volunteeer is goal-directed. The goal is the patient. Whether or not she comes in direct contact with the patient she directs her efforts in his direction. We may speak of this as reversing the polarity of life. Here lies the essence of maturity. The infant grasps for himself, the mature person directs his energy outward for the good of others. Satisfying the needs of patients within the measure of her resources and the definition of her role becomes her obsession.

While it is hardly likely that any volunteer, busy in her work at the hospital, envisions herself as having such saintly status, nonetheless, the concept is an understandable one. The volunteer today is working by and large, not because of social demands or because it is the proper thing to do. She is working as a volunteer because she wants to do this—because she wants to make a contribution in a meaningful way to her community and because she wants to increase the meaning within her own life.

Perhaps such motivation sounds a bit lofty and idealistic. This is not to say that every hospital volunteer is the most highly motivated person or a person who is shortly to be cannonized.

But by and large, the volunteer meets these high standards. And it is with this concept in mind, that the successful volunteer program must be conceived and carried out.

It is the responsibility of the board and hospital administration to recognize the differing motivation of the volunteer's work in the hospital. It must recognize this in setting up programs.

The hospital must recognize that the volunteer has an entirely different motivation from that of the salaried employee just as the employee views the hospital in a different manner than the physician on the medical staff.

The hospital board and administration must impress upon

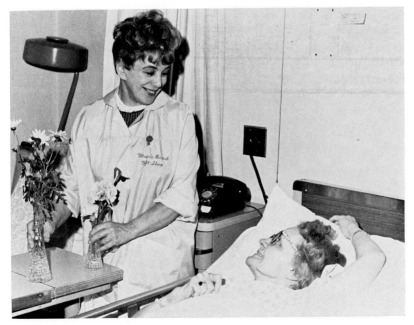

FIGURE 3. Fresh flowers can be a great morale booster for a lonely patient. At this hospital, volunteers get flowers from a floral shop and distribute them to patients. (Photo, Mt. Sinai Hospital, Chicago.)

both employees and medical staff that the volunteer is an essential member of the hospital team. The volunteer can be no more effective than the cooperation and acceptance of other members of the hospital team.

In turn, the volunteer must be properly screened, trained and oriented to this concept of volunteer work, to the individual hospital and to the particular job. To do other than this would be a great disservice to the hospital, its patients, the employees and to the volunteer.

Mutual acceptance depends upon mutual respect and understanding. This must begin at the top—that is, with the trustees—proceed through administration and continue at all levels of the hospital. Only then can a hospital truly hope to have an effective volunteer program.

Chapter IV

ORGANIZING A VOLUNTEER GROUP

IT IS SAID THAT the fashionable women of Boston don't buy their hats—they have their hats. It is also true that most hospitals don't have to worry about organizing auxiliaries—they have their auxiliaries.

But for the hospital which has an auxiliary devoted to fund raising and wishes to organize a service group, or for the hospital planning to organize a service group for the first time, or for a new hospital, this chapter will seek to provide guidance.

The background, organization and formation of the Service League of Lutheran General Hospital, located in the Chicago suburb of Park Ridge, will be sketched here. This Service League was selected because of the authors' familiarity with it and because it has demonstrated over the years some of the things which a service-minded group can do for the hospital and the people the hospital serves.

The roots of the Service League go back to the time when the initial fund raising campaign was begun for a new hospital. Women volunteered and were recruited to help in the community-wide campaign to solicit funds for the building. Some women worked in the fund raising offices, helping prepare materials and mailings. Others of them served on committees for solicitations and helped to conduct the door-to-door campaign.

From this group, came the nucleus of the organization which was to develop. Under the direction of one of the women, a "canteen" was organized to serve meals and snacks to the workmen constructing the hospital. Volunteers were solicited from area churches. Women pitched in to make casseroles, pies and cakes and to serve the meals, coffee and snacks to the construction workers.

It was an excellent project. Many women who wanted to do something to help the new hospital had a chance to participate. Those who had small children would prepare baked goods at home. Since the new hospital was located a considerable distance from any restaurants, it provided a service to the workers (who undoubtedly preferred the home-made pies and cakes to the store-purchased variety) and at the same time it netted a sizable profit for the hospital.

As women heard about the "canteen," many called to see if they could help. Those who did not work at the canteen, aided the fund raising efforts through mailings, office work and similar tasks. Others organized a speakers' bureau to talk to clubs and civic groups.

About eight months before the hospital was scheduled to open, the hospital board of trustees took action to formally organize the group. Among the decisions made by the trustees at this time were:

1. That the Service League would be an integral part of the hospital organization under the sponsorship of the hospital and under the jurisdiction of the hospital's board of trustees.

2. There would be one unified volunteer organization.

3. All members would pay dues.

4. The emphasis would be on service.

5. All members would be tested before being assigned to serve.

6. Volunteer service in the hospital would be directed by a professional staff, selected by the hospital administration and reporting to the hospital administration.

It was with this philosophy in mind that the trustees selected the first Service League board, drawing primarily on those who had been active in the early stages of the hospital. The first board was made up of a president, first vice president and program chairman, second vice president and projects chairman, treasurer, financial secretary, recording secretary, corresponding secretary, membership chairman, memorial fund chairman, social chairman, hospitality chairman, hours and service chairman, junior volunteers chairman and bylaws chairman.

This board then drew up plans for organizing the Service

League. A general information meeting was planned and publicized. Plans for the hospital service league were detailed at the meeting and a date set for the formal organizational meeting. Some 200 women became charter members.

As construction neared completion, plans for a public open house were made with the Service League handling most of the details. At about the same time, a professional director of volunteer services was hired by the hospital.

IN-SERVICE WORK

Under the director's guidance, plans were organized for the volunteers to work in the hospital when it opened. The first job for which the volunteers assumed responsibility was the reception desk. The volunteer director began a pattern of operation which is still continued.

She worked at the reception desk, noting the type of work needed, the types of problems encountered and the general aspects of the job. Based on this knowledge and on consultation with the supervisor of the area, she wrote a job description, trained workers and saw that it was working smoothly.

Then the second area of responsibility was begun, following the same pattern of operation. At the end of the first month, volunteers were working in four areas of the hospital: the reception desk, the doctors' reception area, pediatrics and the control desks on the patient floors.

By the time the hospital had been open one year, volunteers were working in twenty-seven areas of the hospital. In addition to the areas mentioned above, other areas of service included physical therapy aide, pharmacy, patient library, employee health service, checking patient menus, aiding in pastoral care, making puppets for pediatrics and setting up a junior volunteer program.

Educational programs were set up to provide specialized training for volunteers who were capable and interested. (Among them, for example, volunteers were trained to take electrocardiograms and for some time ran the department entirely with volunteer help.)

The first community service project got underway with a

diabetes detection program. By the end of the first year, close to 40,000 hours of volunteer service had been recorded.

Each time a new job for volunteers was planned, it was evaluated by the director and discussed with administration. Generally, it was also discussed with the Service League board and heads of the departments to be served.

Each time the pattern was the same: working at the job by the volunteer director; a writing of the job description, orientation and training.

In line with the decision of the trustees of the hospital, each potential volunteer was required to take the Minnesota Multiphasic Index Test. These results were evaluated by a clinical psychologist with the results passed along to the director of volunteers who used this information in helping assign volunteers to particular jobs.

The testing gave valuable insight to the volunteer on her own self-image. It made the volunteer aware of her own values. It also provided knowledge of the leadership and business capabilities of the volunteers—qualities which some of the volunteers never thought they possessed.

BOARD ORGANIZATION

During this period when the in-service aspects of the volunteer program were being started, the Service League board of directors was also busy.

The board met monthly with the hospital administrator and the volunteer director in attendance. Steps were taken to set the organization up on a strong legal and sound financial basis.

The Service League was incorporated as a not-for-profit organization by the state and was certified by the Internal Revenue Service as being qualified to receive tax-deductible gifts. Officers handling funds were bonded and arrangements were made for an outside audit of the Service League books. Guidelines were established by the board of trustees on how funds could be spent.

Four general membership meetings were scheduled each year with a strong emphasis on education of membership on hospital health matters. A monthly newsletter was started, written and edited by the publicity (later public relations) chairman of the Service League board.

A gift shop was begun in the hospital to provide patients, employees and visitors with sundry items. Vending machines were set up in the hospital under the sponsorship of the Service League.

The basic philosophy of Service League fund raising began to make itself felt: that service was the first consideration with the funds raised being a by-product. As a result, during the first year, the Service League began making television sets available on a rental basis and arranged to have photos taken of all newborn babies.

This was the basic format of events during the first year of operation as a hospital Service League. At the end of the first year of the hospital, 400 volunteers had provided 40,000 hours of service in twenty-seven areas of the hospital ranging from the reception desk to running the entire electrocardiogram department.

The Service League had demonstrated it was not only an integral part of the new hospital, but it was an essential part.

SUMMARY

Obviously, the tracing of the history of any volunteer group would have many similarities as well as some striking differences. Again, what worked for one organization may be totally unsuited for another hospital.

However, certain principles detailed above could be studied and practiced by any hospital service group. These would include the following:

1. Strong support, approval and backing of the hospital board of trustees.

2. Close liaison with the hospital administration.

3. A structured board.

4. A salaried professional volunteer director.

These four elements are essential for any successful program. True, perhaps a good volunteer program can exist without one or two of these four. But a good program can be made better if all four of these points exist.

Chapter V

RELATING TO THE HOSPITAL STAFF

IF THERE IS A cardinal rule for a volunteer, it is this: the volunteer is a part of the hospital—she isn't the whole hospital. The volunteer who can keep this in mind will be a highly successful volunteer, a credit to herself, a source of help to the patient and a greatly appreciated member of the hospital team.

Perhaps the most difficult task a volunteer has is that of adjusting to her role in the hospital. In her regular life, she may be the wife of the city's biggest industrialist, the wife of the president of the medical staff or a highly paid career woman. But when she dons the volunteer uniform, she is also putting on a uniform of anonymity.

A patient could care less if she is Mrs. Big in the community. A head nurse could care less if the volunteer's husband earns more in a month than the nurse earns in a year. As a volunteer, she is there to serve the hospital, the patients and the community. The volunteer who keeps this in mind will be a great asset.

RELATING TO TRUSTEES

Individually a volunteer will have little opportunity to relate to the hospital's governing board. Collectively, however, volunteers will have a great deal to do with the trustees.

First, volunteers will represent one of the major contributors to the hospital. As one of the major contributors, the voice of the volunteer will be heard. True, the volunteers should not expect to run the hospital. (And if they start trying to do so, the trustees should put a stop to it immediately.)

A workable solution should be determined so that the volunteer organization can make its voice heard at the board level.

30

From the trustees' point of view, the volunteer organization is a part of the total hospital picture. From a practical point of view, it is probably less important in the eyes of the trustees than the medical staff and the hospital personnel. True, a wise trustee would never say this aloud, but from a practical point of view, this is probably true.

It is a wise board of trustees which sets up guidelines for the volunteer organization. There is no need for uniformity here. A wise board of trustees retains control of all operations of the hospital as it has been legally and morally charged to do. A board may exercise this trusteeship through the right to approve all by-laws.

It may do this by approving the appointment of officers. It may do this by having a veto power on expenditures. It may do so through a combination of these methods.

A volunteer organization should recognize that the trustees have ultimate authority on all hospital matters. It should seek to find ways to cooperate with the board, rather than seek to cause a conflict.

If volunteers and trustees can continue to keep in mind that they are all working for the same goal—the good of the hospital— there is little likelihood that conflict will develop. It is only when one or both parties puts its own interests ahead of the hospital that problems and conflicts begin to develop. Wise volunteers and wise trustees should be ever alert to prevent this from occurring.

RELATING TO ADMINISTRATION

The running of the hospital has been delegated by the board of trustees to an administrator. It is the administrator who has the day-to-day responsibility for running the hospital. It is the administrator who has the day-to-day responsibility for seeing that volunteers fit into the hospital's work.

The hospital administrator should have the following authority:

1. Right to hire and fire the director of volunteers just as he

holds the same managerial responsibility for other department heads.

2. The right to say where volunteers will be working in the hospital, which jobs they hold and the type of service expected of them.

3. The right to sit in on all board and committee meetings of the formal volunteer organization.

The director of volunteers, as discussed in chapter VIII, is a professional hospital department head, fully responsible to the hospital administrator. The director of volunteers should be paid by the hospital.

The president of the volunteer organization should also have access to the administrator on a regular basis. She may, for various reasons, wish to meet the administrator alone. Regardless, the channels of communication should be kept open between both the administrator and volunteer director and between the administrator and volunteer president.

RELATING TO PROFESSIONAL STAFF

In the years gone by, there was a nagging fear in the minds of many professional staff members that the volunteer might be "doing them out of a job." Fortunately, this is no longer a fear in these days of acute shortages of practically all skilled professionals.

The professional—be it registered nurse, social worker, physical therapist or medical technologist—recognizes that the volunteer is not a threat, but a valuable ally. In this day of acute shortage of personnel, the volunteer is welcomed in practically every segment of the hospital. In fact, many volunteer directors report their biggest complaint from hospital personnel comes from the fact that not enough volunteers are available in the areas of the hospital where they are wanted.

The volunteer has a special job when working in professional areas of the hospital. She may be a college graduate and may be fifty years old, while the professional has a two-year diploma and is a mere twenty years old. Yet, the volunteer must defer to the professional.

A successful volunteer program develops when the volunteers recognize that they are members of the team but are not the whole team. When the volunteer can accept this concept that she is a team member, not a team leader, then a volunteer program is well on its way toward a successful working relationship with the hospital staff.

A volunteer assigned to work in an area where she'll be serving with skilled professionals will need special orientation and preparation for this job. For her not to have this orientation and training would be a distinct disservice to the volunteer, the hospital staff and to the patients.

This is a two-way street. The volunteer needs orientation on working with professionals. The professionals, on the other hand, need orientation on working with volunteers.

It is a wise hospital policy which, as part of its orientation program, be it formal or informal, provides a time for the volunteer director to speak to new employees on the role of the volunteer. A volunteer can be only as effective as her acceptance in a particular area of the hospital. This acceptance will come only if new employees are informed fully about the role of the volunteer.

This information should not only specify what volunteers do in the hospital, but it should also stress that volunteers are essential members of the hospital team, that they are where they are because this is a directive of administration and a policy of the board.

Usually, there is no problem, since most areas of the hospital are glad to have the extra hands available. Just as the best medicine is preventive medicine, so the best way to solve a problem with volunteers in the hospital setting is to avoid having the problem occur in the first place.

The volunteer should remember that the hospital is a complex team operation, involving the close cooperation of dozens of different occupational groups. When a volunteer dons her uniform, she also assumes an obligation to give of her time and talents for the benefits of others. This attitude should be reflected in her dealings with all she comes in contact with—physicians, patients, visitors, employees and other volunteers. This attitude must be constantly stressed to all volunteers during recruitment and orientation, in publications and in every communications media available.

FORMAL AND INFORMAL RELATIONS

There are two basic frames of reference in referring to volunteer relations. First, there is the relationship of the formal volunteer group to the hospital. Second, there is the relationship of the individual volunteer to the hospital.

Both the group and the individual must maintain good rapport since a poor performance by one volunteer reflects on the entire organization. In turn the attitude of the entire group can make things difficult for the work of the individual volunteer in her work.

Volunteers in many hospitals have a certain degree of anonymity. Since they usually come in to the hospital for only a few hours per week, they may not get to know as many people as a full-time employee does. Yet, the individual volunteer may be the only volunteer which a patient, visitor or employee comes in contact with. As a result, the entire volunteer group may be judged on what one volunteer does.

Obviously if she makes a good impression, the reputation of the entire organization is enhanced. If she makes a poor impression, it can do great harm not only to the volunteer organization, but to the entire concept of volunteer services. A volunteer is a member of a chain, which is only as strong as its weakest link.

Chapter VI

THE ORGANIZATION OF A
VOLUNTEER BOARD

THE GOVERNING OF the volunteer group should be vested in a board of directors. This board should be under the jurisdiction of the hospital's trustees since the trustees have the legal and moral responsibility for the total operation of the hospital.

Officers for the volunteer board can be selected in a number of ways. Some groups elect them by a membership vote. Others have the main officers appointed by the trustees with the remaining directors selected by the officers. Still others use a combination of these methods.

It does not make a great deal of difference how the officers are selected. Arguments can be made for and against any method. It is important that the board members selected have a clear understanding of their jobs, that they recognize their position is to help the hospital (not to further social ambitions) and that their selection was based on their interest, ability and desire to help rather than as an honor to them or a tribute to their popularity.

This chapter is designed to provide in greater detail the role of the board collectively and of individual positions on the board.

FUNCTIONS OF THE TOTAL BOARD

The board of the volunteer group has the legal and moral responsibility for directing and guiding the formal organization of the group. It does so with the understanding that its actions are reportable to and accountable to the hospital administration and trustees.

The board should meet regularly at a stated time and a

stated place. It is better that the board meet in the hospital itself rather than in a social setting so that the emphasis of the board meeting will be on business.

The board should have a written constitution and by-laws which have approval of the hospital's trustees. It is also a good idea for the organization to be legally incorporated.

List of "do's" for the volunteer group and board:

1. Do be business-like in the board meetings.
2. Do be incorporated.
3. Do have a written agenda.
4. Do have limitations on the length of service for board members.
5. Do keep the board representative.

And equally important, a list of "don'ts" for the board:

1. Don't let one group dominate the board (for example, wives of trustees, doctors, major donors, etc.).
2. Don't forget that the major objective of the organization is service to the hospital and the people it serves.
3. Don't let the election of president and other officers become a popularity contest.
4. Don't let the board meeting become a social event. (But they all don't have to be stodgy either.)
5. Don't let the board (or individual officers) do the job for which the director of volunteers is hired.

COMPOSITION AND DUTIES OF OFFICERS

Each volunteer board will have a little different composition. However, most boards will have officers and chairmen with assigned duties. We list below some of the most commonly used titles along with a brief description for each officer which could be adapted for a majority of situations. Each board should have a written job description for each board member.

President: The president is the chief executive officer of the organization, presides at all meetings, acts as a liaison between the organization and trustees and administrator, represents the organization at public events and meetings, fills board vacancies which may occur and works closely with the director of volunteers.

President-elect: (Also called first vice president or executive vice president.) The president-elect sits as a member of the executive committee, will become president when term of current president expires, will succeed president if president leaves office before expiration of term, and acts for president when president cannot attend.

Offices of other vice presidents such as first, second and third vice presidents can be established if the need arises. On a large board (twenty or more members) the several vice presidents may be assigned certain areas of responsibilities. For example, the first vice president could be in charge of certain areas of the board responsibility such as awards, junior volunteers, etc. The second vice president could have the responsibility for public relations, memorial fund, etc. The need for additional vice presidents depends in large part on the local situation, size of the group, scope of activities and related items of this nature.

Secretary: The board may have several secretaries or the duties may be combined in one office. If the duties are divided, this is one method of doing it.

Recording Secretary: This secretary acts as the legal secretary of the board, signing the necessary legal documents, takes care of the corporate seal and related legal items. She also takes minutes of the board and general meetings, handles the secretarial duties associated with these meetings and the other typical duties of the secretary. She may also be charged with such responsibilities as maintaining the historical files, serving as a member of the executive committee and keeping the organization's standing policies.

Corresponding Secretary: This secretary handles all general correspondence for the organization including the mailing of meeting notices, writing the thank you letters and acknowledgments and related duties.

Treasurer: She handles all cash receipts of the organization, and pays for all approved bills. She prepares regular financial statements, submits any necessary tax payments and maintains the necessary financial records as required by the hospital and state and federal taxing bodies. She, like other members of the board who handle money, should be bonded.

Financial Secretary: This may be combined with the treasurer's job, but in a larger organization should be a separate position. The financial secretary works closely with the treasurer. She is responsible for billing and collecting membership dues and maintaining the needed records. She may also be in charge of all billing done by the organization (such as television rental and similar things).

DIRECTORS

The remaining members of the board can be either at-large members or have specific assignments. Among these specific duties could be the following:

Junior Volunteers Director: This director should provide the guidance for the junior volunteer program. She should work closely with the director of volunteers in the promotion, training and scheduling of the junior volunteers (if the volunteer staff does not do this). She should also handle arrangements for recognition and awards for the junior volunteers.

Health Careers Chairman: Many times this job is combined with the junior volunteer chairman. She should work to stimulate interest in health careers among junior volunteers, be in charge of any health career scholarships awarded by the group, and actively work to promote the concept of health careers among junior volunteers and within the community.

Volunteer Awards Chairman: This chairman should be in charge of seeing that the appropriate pins, certificates, etc., are available for presentation to the volunteers who have served the required hours as set by the group's policies. She should be chairman of the program at which awards are made, handle the arrangements, etc. She may also be in charge of keeping track of the hours given by volunteers or this duty may be handled by a separate chairman.

Benefits and Projects Director: If the organization sponsors special benefits (plays, concerts, etc.) this person should be in charge of these benefits. She should serve as chairman of the benefit committee, arranging for the promotion and sale of tickets, donations and arrangements of the event itself. By the nature of her position, she should maintain close liaison with the hospital's fund raising department (if one exists).

Memorial Fund Director: If the group sponsors a memorial (or remembrance fund) this chairman should arrange for the collection of memorial gifts, notification of families for whom memorials were given, providing receipts to the donors and similar items. She should also arrange for suitable printed materials to be prepared. (For more information, see chapter XIV on fund raising.)

Program Director: This chairman should have the responsibility for arranging the program at general and special membership meetings of the service group. She should also be in charge of all physical arrangements for the meetings.

Public Relations Chairman: This chairman should arrange for the appropriate news stories and photographs of volunteer events to be provided for internal and external publicity. She should also take the responsibility for writing and editing the volunteer publication. She should work closely with the hospital's public relations department. (For practical guidance, she should consult the book *Public Relations for Hospitals.*)

Social Director: This chairman has the basic responsibility for the social aspects of the group, ranging from seeing that there is coffee at the board meetings to the arrangement of the more elegant affairs which the group may have from time to time.

These directors could fit into the vast majority of service organizations. Obviously, this is not an all-inclusive list. For special projects and enterprises, specialized directors can be established.

For example, if the organization runs a gift shop, it is logical that there would be a board-level person acting as chairman. The same thing could be true of a resale shop, a snack shop and other enterprises.

If the organization is new, a recruitment and membership chairman might be necessary. If the group is community-minded, a community service chairman could be included.

The thing an organization should keep in mind as it sets up a formal board is flexibility—the flexibility both to add new positions and drop existing ones as the need arises or as times change.

In addition to the above officers, the board should also have as ex officio members, the hospital administrator (or designated assistant administrator depending upon the size of the hospital), the director of volunteers and the trustees volunteer committee chairman. All of these should have full rights of the floor; although they are not voting members.

The volunteer board should also remember that the director of volunteers is an employee of the hospital, responsible to the hospital administrator, not the volunteer board. Things such as the director's salary, work load, staff and duties are not determined by the volunteer board.

It is the function of the board to set policy, not to run the hospital or the volunteer program. When members of the board recognize this, the entire hospital benefits.

A volunteer board which starts trying to run the entire hospital does itself a disservice and does the hospital and the people it serves an even greater injustice.

Chapter VII

IN-SERVICE EDUCATION FOR VOLUNTEERS

A GOOD VOLUNTEER program must be constantly changing and improving if it is to keep pace with the modern hospital. As a volunteer program changes and improves, an on-going program of education is needed.

If the volunteer group is to keep its best members, the group must continue to offer challenges. Some volunteers will be happy and content to do the same job year after year. Others will seek the challenge of learning new tasks.

In turn, as the volunteer organization progresses, it will add new programs which will involve education and training. This can range from simple on-the-job training by one volunteer of another to a formal educational program with training by doctors and other professional personnel.

Let us look at some examples. As discussed in previous chapters, the good volunteer director is constantly alert seeking new ways in which volunteers can serve the hospital.

Let us say that the hospital's medical director has heard that in some hospitals volunteers have been trained to take electro-cardiagrams. "Could such a program be done here?" he wonders. He asks the questions of the director of volunteers.

After discussing the question at length (including involve-ment of the hospital administrator), plans are made to investigate it further. The director of volunteers will see if there are volun-teers who are interested. The medical director finds out the feelings of the medical staff and handles arrangements for teaching.

From this beginning, a new program is undertaken. After securing the needed agreement, a pilot program is begun. A cardiologist provides the basic instruction, teaching not only the basics of electrocardiography, but also teaching the basics of heart disease, working with heart patients and similar topics. EKG technicians, eager to have more help, aid in the instructional program, showing upkeep of equipment, copying and mounting of EKG tapes and other procedures.

The course of instruction is structured. Lectures and training are held at definite times for a specified number of weeks. Testing and review are part of the curriculum. Volunteers are required to attend all lectures. Those completing the course receive certificates presented by the hospital administrator.

This program has the elements of a good training program. There is a genuine desire on the part of the hospital and its staff to have the program. It meets a genuine need within the hospital. It offers a challenge to the volunteer.

Like most good programs, it requires the cooperation of a number of segments of the hospital for success. The director of volunteers, the medical staff, the hospital administrator and the hospital personnel—all have to cooperate and join together to insure success.

As is the case in all good volunteer programs, everyone benefits: the patient and the doctor because there is now better coverage available, the hospital personnel because there are more skilled hands to help, the hospital administrator because there is now one less area of personnel shortage to worry about, and the volunteer who has a challenging job awaiting her.

This is one example. There are others.

Let us say that a hospital has a shortage of nurses aides. The question is asked, "Could volunteers be trained to help here?"

The same procedure would follow: discussion with the administrator, talks with the nursing staff, recruitment from the volunteers and training by the professional staff. In this case, training would be handled by an in-service instructor of the nursing staff rather than by the physician.

Other examples could be cited. It really doesn't matter where the idea originated, whether the director of nursing goes to the director of volunteers or the director of volunteers goes to the director of nursing. The important thing is that the idea is carried through the established channels, that people be involved and that adequate training be provided.

Properly trained people are essential to the well-being of the hospital and the people it serves. This applies as much to volunteers as it does to paid personnel.

On areas discussed here such as nursing and electrocardiography, the director of volunteers must and should rely on the professionals in the field to provide the training. The director can assist in planning and give guidance on the level of materials used, but she doesn't have the technical competence to teach such programs.

The director of volunteers will find that most teaching and training will not require the service of medical professionals. Most of the training will have to be done by the director herself.

Now it may be that the director comes from a teaching or personnel background so setting up teaching and training programs will be simple. But chances are quite good that she doesn't have these skills. As a result, she's going to have to learn how to do these things.

HOW TO TEACH

One important aspect of volunteer teaching is that most of it will be done on a one-to-one basis in an informal setting. As a result, the director will not have to be concerned with highly structured lectures and elaborately worked out lesson plans.

Yet, this does not mean the director must rely on old-fashioned methods of teaching. The volunteer director will be wise if she utilizes the resources available in the hospital.

An increasing number of hospitals are installing closed-circuit television systems with video taping. This provides a tool which has great potential for teaching volunteers.

Let us say a volunteer is being trained to work at the main reception desk. This is the nerve center of the hospital and while most of those stopping at the desk merely seek a room number, anything can happen there. The volunteers at this desk must be well trained.

To instruct a new volunteer for this position, typical situations could be filmed and shown. The new volunteer could also be filmed so she can get an idea of what sort of an impression she makes to the public.

Georgia Regional Hospital, Atlanta, has used video tapes to train more than 800 volunteers. One taped program shows a day in the life of the volunteer. Included are such things as the volunteer signing in, reporting to the nursing station and doing the assigned tasks. Special lectures for volunteers are also taped by the appropriate professional and then shown to the volunteer as the need arises.

According to Dr. Aubrey Daniels, director of the hospital's department of psychology, who helped develop the program, there are two major advantages in using video tape:

1. Volunteers can come to the hospital at their convenience for orientation and training.

2. All volunteers receive this valuable orientation and training.

Other video programs are used as a continuing program of in-service education for other volunteers.

Closed circuit television systems are now within the price range of almost all hospitals. If the hospital does not have such a system, it may be that a nearby school or industry will make its facilities available.

Of course, while video taping is highly useful, it is not the only audiovisual tool which can be used.

One of the most useful, easy-to-use and inexpensive audiovisual teaching devices is the overhead projector. This can be effectively utilized for one or two people or for a large group. It has an advantage in that materials can be prepared and then used again and again for repeated presentations such as basic orientation. Studies show that there is a much greater degree of retention when audiovisuals are combined with a person just talking.

Every hospital should have an overhead projector. Any dealer will be glad to demonstrate how to use such a piece of equipment. They are inexpensive enough that a volunteer office can have one of its own if it wishes.

Such devices as flip charts and bulletin boards can also be

used. For more elaborate presentation, a 35 mm slide presentation may be developed.

The purpose of this section is not to make the director of volunteers an expert on audiovisuals or to qualify her for a teaching certificate. Rather, it is to help her realize that there are many tools available for use in training programs.

We have been dealing here with specific education—that is, education or training for a specific task or job. To do her job adequately, the volunteer must be trained in the specific areas of responsibility. She knows the why and wherefore of the reception desk, the rules of the pediatric department and visiting hours on the maternity floor.

In addition to specific training for a specified job, the volunteer must receive training in the hospital itself. Most of this training will be on a less formal and a less direct method of teaching. Yet, it is equally important as the training for the job.

MEETINGS

Most meetings of volunteer groups are a waste of time. They are spent reading minutes and discussing minutiae; they are social events, or they are programs totally unrelated to that which volunteers should have the most interest in—the hospital.

Oriental flower arranging or a review of the best seller may have a certain amount of interest. But the volunteer group is organized for people interested in the hospital, not people interested in oriental flower arranging or in best sellers.

The hospital abounds with interesting programs which can be fascinating to the membership and instructive at the same time.

Why are coronary care unit costs twice as much as the regular hospital room? A program on this topic can answer this question and also give highly interesting and important information on the life-saving care provided by such a facility.

Good programs don't just happen. They must be prepared well in advance. The volunteer group should work closely with the administrator, medical director and others.

Here are a dozen good program topics which would be available in almost any hospital.

1. What to do when a child is poisoned. (Presented by the hospital pharmacist and emergency room staff.)
2. We've come a long way since Florence Nightingale. (Presented by the nursing staff.)
3. The hospital of tomorrow. (Presented by the hospital administrator.)
4. We don't call them x-ray any more. (Presented by the radiologist.)
5. The hospital you don't see. (Presented by the chief engineer.)
6. We never stop cleaning house. (Presented by the executive housekeeper.)
7. When a child enters the hospital. (Presented by the pediatrics staff.)
8. The longest shopping list in town. (Presented by the hospital's purchasing agent.
9. Use and abuse of the emergency department. (Presented by the emergency room staff.)
10. How the medical staff is organized. (Presented by the medical director.)
11. What the hospital dollar buys. (Presented by the administration.)
12. Why I am a trustee. (Presented by the president of the board.)

Properly planned programs can pack people in at the meetings. Topics of this nature cannot only be highly interesting but also highly informative. And a well-informed volunteer is a better volunteer.

NEWSLETTERS

Most volunteer groups have a periodic newsletter. Most are poorly done. They contain a hodge-podge of promotion for coming fund-raising events, reports of previous fund-raising events, poems, beautiful thoughts and gossipy chatter. Few contain information which contributes to the educative process of the volunteer.

This doesn't mean that the volunteer newsletter has to be

dull or pedantic. Information on the hospital and its program can be presented in a light and interesting manner. Properly used the volunteer newsletter is a useful tool of education and communication. Improperly used, it is a waste of time, paper and postage.

OUTSIDE EVENTS

Volunteers should be encouraged to attend outside meetings, conventions and seminars. Most state and local hospital associations have special meetings for volunteers. Leadership seminars are offered by colleges and university extension services. The volunteer group should send its leaders, present and future, to these types of meetings whenever possible.

Volunteers meeting with other volunteers is a highly useful way of sharing ideas. The good volunteer is always seeking to learn. It is up to the hospital to do the teaching.

SUMMARY

Education takes many forms. It can be in formal classes; it can be in an informal method through programs and newsletters.

When education is on-going the volunteer can provide the maximum service to the hospital.

Chapter VIII

THE ROLE OF THE DIRECTOR

THE SALARIED PROFESSIONAL director of volunteers is a recent addition to the hospital family. A decade ago, she was totally unknown in all but a few of the largest, most progressive hospitals. In 1969, an estimated 1500 hospitals had salaried directors, with this number growing each month.

A director of volunteers finds herself in a somewhat curious role in the hospital setting. Most of her colleagues have exacting educational requirements. A nurse adds R.N. after her name only after taking the prescribed courses and passing the required state examinations. It's the same for the physician, physical therapist, administrator, radiologic technologist and a whole host of other hospital occupations.

A person seeking to become director of volunteers could not take a college program if she wanted to do so. There are no educational requirements for the position.

Ten directors were asked about their educational and background experience for the position. Of the ten, one had a bachelor degree, four had some college and five had no college education. Of these same ten, all had been very interested and active in civic affairs, all loved working with people, most had been ardent church workers and four had been working in hospitals in other areas, such as assistant in public relations, secretary to an administrator, social worker and head of admitting.

This in no way is meant to be a representative sampling of volunteer directors. It is fairly safe to say that any group would show a similarly wide variety of backgrounds in education and experience.

A hospital seeking to hire a director of volunteers faces a problem. Since no colleges teach the subject, an administrator can't recruit through a college. He, of course, can advertise in a hospital journal and seek a director wanting to make a change or an assistant director wanting to move up.

Most administrators, however, look to their own communities when seeking to hire a director of volunteers. Since there are no formal requirements for the hospital, what should he look for as he searches for a director? Here's a check list which can serve as a guide:

1. She should have experience in working with people. This could include industrial or hospital personnel work, guidance counseling or social work. It could be a more informal community work such as scouts, PTA and church groups. However, a word of caution—just because a person has been active in organizations doesn't guarantee competence in the position.

2. The person should have demonstrated organizational and leadership abilities. One hint for new hospitals: a woman who has successfully helped organize a fund drive is a likely candidate to consider.

3. She should have the ability to relate to people.

4. She should genuinely like people and have the ability to understand and work with all types of people on professional as well as lay levels.

5. She should have enthusiasm.

6. She should have that rather indefinable quality of charisma.

7. She may or may not have been active in the hospital's auxiliary. (Sometimes not having been active is a distinct advantage.)

8. She should have demonstrated imagination.

9. She should have a reasonably good business knowledge and sense.

10. She should be aware and sensitive to the needs of others.

Of course, any administrator who finds a person with all of these characteristics should hire her immediately—she could probably handle any job in the hospital including the presidency of the board of trustees.

However, a good administrator recognizes that no one person

can have all of these qualities. But he should strive to find someone with as many of them as possible.

In searching for someone, the administrator should watch for pitfalls of this nature:

1. Hiring someone who may not have much talent, experience or knowledge, but is a "pleasant person whom everyone adores."

2. He should avoid placing someone in the position just because the person is available or needs a new position in the hospital family. (A former executive housekeeper may make a good director of volunteers, but she should be selected for the position because of her abilities not merely because the hospital is going to contract housekeeping and the administrator does not want to have to fire the former executive housekeeper.)

3. The administrator is tempting fate when he hires someone too close to the hospital family such as a trustee's wife, the auxiliary president or a physician's wife. It may work out, but the administrator should be warned that he's walking on dangerous ground.

If the administrator wants a dynamic volunteer program, he should be sure he hires a director who has demonstrated the ability to put plans into practice.

RESPONSIBILITY OF THE DIRECTOR

Auxiliaries are reminded frequently that they must be concerned, that they must not isolate themselves from other health groups or agencies in the community, that they must support efforts to meet the community's health needs and become involved in comprehensive planning and in regional medical programs.

One of a leader's primary responsibilities is to demonstrate this concern, to keep it constantly before volunteers and to help them find creative ways to act on their concern. She is charged with making volunteers aware of the need to examine their shortcomings and to take action. The leader's role, in addition to the teaching mentioned earlier, is that of designer, explorer and discoverer. A leader need not create any "grand design"—she only sees wants and needs before others do, then prepares ways to help attain results. She opens new vistas for the realization of potentialities and for creative expression for personal and group fulfillment.

The self-examination the director recommends for volunteers should be practiced by herself as well. How can she determine if she is functioning creatively? Asking herself some of the following questions might help:

1. Am I an autocratic leader or one who uses the method that fits the situation?

2. Do I see myself as solely responsible for the growth of the volunteer program, or do I involve an increasing number in this responsibility?

3. Do I try to superimpose one solution, approach, or decision, or do I understand that the experience of one group in making a decision or carrying out a project is not always the right one for all groups? (Such experiences can, it is true, serve as guidelines for other groups.)

4. Do I consider myself an enforcer of authority, or am I developing and motivating higher standards for planning and performance?

As creative leaders execute their responsibilities, they will be part of today's viable, exciting and rapidly changing health field. They will put forth their best efforts to lead with skill and intelligence, with enthusiasm and imagination. With such an attitude, they will stimulate others to become more creative. They will find new joy in service and new opportunity for personal growth.

Best of all, volunteers will find more constructive ways to serve their communities, and all involved will have a sense of having made some real advancement toward accomplishing a splendid purpose.

ON HIRING A DIRECTOR

A question which will often come up before trustees and an administrator is, Can the hospital afford a director of volunteers? Perhaps it is just as logical for the board to ask, Can the hospital afford not to have a director of volunteers? It is true that some rather successful volunteer programs operate with a nonsalaried volunteer chairman or coordinator. A very small hospital or a hospital with only a few volunteers available may not need nor be able to afford a director.

Yet, many hospitals of one hundred or fewer beds find that a salaried director of volunteers is a good investment. A volunteer program, like any other aspect of the hospital is only as good as the people guiding and directing it. A hospital which seeks to have a good volunteer program will seek out and hire a director.

Before interviewing for a director, a definite job description should be drawn up. This will be of benefit to the administrator and also help prevent future misunderstandings. If the position includes helping handle hospital fund raising, then spell it out in advance, rather than making it a surprise for the new director. A sample job description is found in the appendix.

DUTIES OF THE DIRECTOR

The director of volunteers is an employee of the hospital, not of the volunteer group itself. Because of this, her job is to work for the hospital, not for the volunteer organization. This should be specifically spelled out and make known to all volunteers and auxiliary members before the director is hired.

What then is the job of the director of volunteers? The director basically plans and organizes, interviews prospective volunteers, conducts orientation and training, places volunteers within the hospital, provides supervision of volunteers on the job, acts as a liaison between the volunteer organization and the hospital, and is also a hospital department head.

Planning

A volunteer program is no better than the planning and organization which precedes it. A director analyzes the duties expected of volunteers, attempting to determine what can be done and, equally important, what cannot be done by volunteers. She talks with department heads and supervisors to determine what they feel a volunteer can do in their respective area. On the basis of this she writes job descriptions.

Let us take a hypothetical case. There is a shortage of help in the offices of the dietary department. Could volunteers be utilized here?, the chief dietitian asks the director of volunteers.

The director spends time in the dietary office observing the work flow. She observes work done on the patient floors by members of the dietetic staff. She talks to dietitians, nurses and clerks.

On the basis of these observations, she and the chief dietitian conclude that volunteers could be utilized most practically on working with patient menus. A job description is written as follows:

JOB DESCRIPTION FOR VOLUNTEERS WORKING ON DIET MENUS

The Dietary Department has a staff of dietitians and diet clerks. The department selects and oversees the preparation of food for the patients, employees and hospital visitors.

This is a description of your duties.

General Procedure for a Volunteer in this Area

I. In the volunteer office you will find the clipboards and diet sheets for the floors. You should have a supply of clips, small note paper and pencils.

Menus are collected from all patient floors.

II. Go to the nurses' stations on the floor where you will find menus in labeled container.

A. Organize the menus:
  1. Arrange them as to room number.
  2. Make sure that the menu has been properly circled by checking the diet sheet (hanging on the wall at the station).
  3. Enter on your sheet the missing menus—type of diet and other remarks.

B. Menu Information:
  1. The following terms may be used and indicate patient does not receive menu.
  1. *Hold*—food withheld for x-ray or other tests

      2. *N.B.O.*—nothing by mouth

      3. *Lqd*—no solids, liquids only

      4. N.P.O.—nothing, postoperative case

      5. $H_2 O$—receiving oxygen

      6. Fasting—not to receive food

  2. *At the bottom of the menu,* food restrictions will be stamped.

    Example: no salt, no sugar or no pepper.

  3. Various colors denote type of diet prescribed by the physician:

    white—general diet

    blue—calculated

    green—bland

    yellow—soft

    pink—low fat, low salt

III. Menu Collection

A. When menus are missing:

  1. If the food cart is still on the floor, check it for menus.

  2. After you have determined which menus are missing, go to the rooms one by one. Knock at the door for admittance. If the doctor is attending the patient or a test is taking place, excuse yourself and return at a more convenient time. The same applies if a member of the clergy is making a visit.

    If the patient is asleep, please do not disturb. In case a patient may be under an oxygen tent, check with the head nurse before you approach that patient.

B. Assisting the patient:

  1. Many patients will have their menus ready. Others will need your help. Call out the menu and circle the patient's selections. Here is where you really are of service.

  2. Some patients are seriously ill, others depressed and many are anxious and lonely. It may take up to 10 minutes to get a selection but give them that time graciously. They truly appreciate your help. The hospital honors requests for special foods. Perhaps a patient may desire a different choice of fruit or juice, etc. See that this is written on the menu, although the final decision is up to the dietitian.

C. "Today's Menus":

  You will be collecting menus for the following day's meals. However, often you will find "today's" menus. If it is for luncheon, take it to the diet clerk before 11:30, or send by pneumatic tube system at control desk on floor.

D. After Collection:
> When you finish collecting all available menus on a floor, go to the dietary offices. Hand menus to diet clerks. When time permits, they will check through their lists. They will also give you menus to take back to those who had "hold" on breakfast. There may be some diet changes, and you return those to the patients on the respective floors.

IV. Refrain from discussing a patient's illness with him or others. Do not purchase candy or other items, if requested, without the approval of the head nurse. There may be restrictions as to use of sugar or tobacco. Work around situations; don't hamper the efforts of those attending a patient. Don't hesitate to ask the nurses if you are in doubt. Write down on paper any complaints or commendations and deliver to the office. In no way make statements to defend the department. The dietitians will handle any complaints or unusual requests.

INTERVIEWING

After checking the job description with the personnel involved to be certain she has covered the major points, the next step is to place the right volunteers in this position. This brings up the next point: Interviewing.

The question in the director's mind when she interviews should be this: Can this volunteer serve the hospital? Initially there is no need to determine anything but this. If the volunteer can, in the opinion of the director, serve the hospital, then the next point to determine is how and where.

Interviewing is probably the major key to a successful program.

It is difficult to provide a sample questionnaire for interviewing prospective volunteers. Each volunteer is an individual and each interview, as a result, will be unique. However, there are certain basic principles which the director can keep in mind as she conducts an interview. (Never do this over the phone.)

1. Allow adequate time. Do not try to rush it through in a few minutes.

2. Use open-ended questions rather than questions which can be answered by "Yes" or "No."

3. Attempt to determine the attitude of the volunteer as to why she is volunteering.

4. Explain in detail what is expected of the volunteer including such items as membership dues, purchase of uniform, wearing of uniforms and related items. Also explain the responsibilities a volunteer must assume in relation to her work.

5. No matter how skilled the director is at interviewing, there are things which she may not discern. As a result, certain types of testing may be used to supplement, not replace interviewing. (For example, some hospitals have used the Minnesota Multi-phasic Index test for all volunteers.)

6. Other considerations would be the applicant's relationships with family, friends and working groups. The art of relating to others in volunteer work is very important.

7. Never turn away applicants with no education, but check to be sure that they are cheerful, courteous, considerate and neat in their dress. These qualities may offset the lack of education.

8. Look for physical handicaps of any kind and be honest in discussion of the deformity. Do not give them a job they are incapable of performing.

9. Make clear to prospective volunteers any benefits the hospital offers or does not offer them, such as meals at a discount.

10. Above all else, be honest with the applicant. This is one way of winning respect. If your honesty gets across to applicant many problems will never arise because they will come to you and feel free to discuss things in the future. Honesty opens the door for good communications between the director and volunteers.

ORIENTATION AND TRAINING

The prospective volunteer has been interviewed and the director feels that she will be a welcome addition to the hospital's volunteer service. It is now up to the director to arrange for orientation and training. As discussed in Chapter VII, a volunteer can be only as good as her training and orientation to the hospital itself and to her specific job assignment.

Most important, however, will be a key decision on the part of the director: placement of the volunteer. Many prospective volunteers come into the hospital with their minds made up as to where they want to serve or where they do not want to serve.

Not every volunteer can serve in pediatrics, on the maternity floor or reception desk, areas which usually rank high in the volunteer popularity poll.

Many subjective decisions must be made by the director as she seeks to fit the new volunteer into the proper post. For example, if the interview gave the director a hint that the prospective volunteer is quite a gossip, the director would try to steer the new volunteer away from areas where confidential information is available.

Did the interview indicate the prospective volunteer might be a bit squeamish? In that case, better keep her away from the emergency room.

Of course, at the same time, the director is also faced with certain problems. Perhaps the most critical need at the moment is help at the reception desk. Perhaps the person is not perfectly suited for the position, but it is also important that the reception desk have coverage. Should the director take the chance and assign the volunteer there?

These are typical of the multitude of problems which the director has as she seeks to fit each person into the right job. Unlike the personnel director, the volunteer director must seek to find a spot for every likely volunteer.

Certainly, no director will "bat 1,000" in her attempts to fit the pegs into the holes. But a successful director must learn to score on a high percentage, otherwise she, the volunteer service and the hospital itself soon may be in trouble.

SUPERVISION

The volunteer director must have both supervision of, and follow-up on, all volunteers. Obviously a director cannot be everywhere at once. Even a moderate-size hospital may have 50 or 100 volunteers working at any given time. Because of this, the director must rely on department heads and supervisors to provide supervision and feedback on volunteers.

This is one key reason why a director of volunteers must maintain exceptional rapport with other areas of the hospital. Without this rapport, it would be difficult if not impossible to maintain supervision and follow-up on volunteers. If a new volunteer is not working out in an assignment, a word from a cooperative department head to the director can help ward off trouble immediately. When this two-way communication exists between the director of volunteers and the hospital department head, a good working relationship with volunteers will also exist. If this relationship doesn't exist, the effectiveness of volunteers will be sharply curtailed.

A FEW CONCLUDING REMARKS

This is a bit of an afterthought directed primarily to the administrator who is seeking to hire a director or to a person who has just taken a position as director of volunteers at a hospital without having previous experience in the field.

Do not be discouraged if all the things outlined in this chapter do not happen immediately. Every good director will make mistakes in the course of doing her job. Because of the nature of her work, she may make similar mistakes more than once.

Being a good volunteer director is a difficult job. It requires the ability to gain psychological insight into a person with the skill of a board-certified psychiatrist.

It requires the ability to fit a person into a position with the adroitness of a vocational counselor.

It requires the tact of a French diplomat.

It requires the ability to teach and instruct with the skill of a Harvard professor.

It requires a person who can remember names and faces with the ability of a Chicago politician.

It is undoubtedly for these reasons that no university is audacious enough to set up a curriculum to train directors of volunteers.

Chapter IX

TEEN-AGE VOLUNTEERS

If it is true that every little girl yearns to be a nurse at some time in her life, it is probably true that every girl wants to be a junior volunteer in the hospital. As a result, recruiting of junior volunteers is generally an easy task. But it is a harder task to make certain that the junior volunteers (and junior volunteers can be boys as well as girls) have a worthwhile, meaningful and important job to do in the hospital.

A great deal has been written and said about the perception of today's young men and women. An equal amount has been written and said about their desire to do something significant with their time. This desire to participate in a meaningful way in their community is highly commendable. It is up to the volunteer program to make certain that the junior volunteers have significant work to do.

From a selfish point of view, hospitals probably have a bigger stake in the junior volunteers than in the senior volunteers. It is the junior volunteers who hopefully will become the nurses, practical nurses, technologists, physicians, physical therapists and the host of other health practitioners so desperately needed. The wise hospital administrator will skillfully utilize the junior volunteer program to acquaint young men and women with the multitude of career possibilities open in the health field.

A junior volunteer program should be set up in such a way that youngsters will become acquainted with a variety of professions and will also have an opportunity to explore in depth that field in which they are especially interested. (Within reason, of course. It doesn't mean that the embryonic brain surgeon should be allowed to run in and out of surgery. But it does mean that he should get a chance to meet and talk to a surgeon at the surgeon's convenience.)

SETTING UP A PROGRAM

The setting up of a junior volunteer program is no different basically than establishing an adult volunteer program. The junior volunteer program should be set up with the advice and consent of the hospital administration.

It should be under the direct supervision of the director of volunteers. If the hospital does not have a salaried volunteer director, the supervision should be delegated to a junior volunteer chairman of the volunteer group board. In either case, rules governing junior volunteers should be set up with the approval of the hospital administrator.

In setting up a program, a number of points should be considered.

First, is the hospital staff truly interested in having junior volunteers? Unless the junior volunteers, are really wanted, a program should not be initiated. For hospitals not attuned to youth, it could be a disturbing influence.

Second, does the hospital have important work for them to do?

Third, has the health career aspect of junior volunteers been carefully planned and programmed?

Fourth, has the hospital administration given its approval and backing?

If the answer is yes to these four questions, then a junior volunteer program should be initiated.

RECRUITING

Usually recruiting will be no problem. Unless there have been unsuccessful programs in the past in the hospital or in other hospitals in the community, there should be no problem in getting recruits.

However, the hospital should be interested in quality as well as quantity. Good junior volunteers don't just happen—

they must be sought and recruited. A sample application blank is found in the appendix:

Here are the sources which are most likely to produce good junior volunteers.

1. Health career clubs in local high schools.

2. Youth groups in churches.

3. Organized youth groups. These can include Boy Scouts, Girl Scouts, Campfire Girls, 4-H Clubs, high school service organizations (such as the Kiwanis-sponsored Key Clubs) and related organizations.

4. The hospital family. This would include children of volunteers, medical staff and employees. (A word of caution: be certain junior volunteers aren't limited to just the children of these groups. The good volunteer program provides a healthy cross-section of the community including minority groups within the community.)

5. Through news and feature stories in local news media about the program.

Generally these sources should provide plenty of volunteers. It is a good idea when starting a program to promote gradually. It is unfortunate and highly detrimental to the hospital if an appeal is made for volunteers and then a large number must be turned down because the hospital cannot accommodate all those who apply.

CRITERIA FOR VOLUNTEERS

Before starting the program, criteria for the junior volunteers should be carefully established. Among the points to be considered are the following:

1. Age. Generally a minimum age of fourteen should be set. In certain institutions, there may be reasons for a fifteen or sixteen year minimum, but fourteen is a good age. The junior volunteer is mature enough for the work, but still not overly involved in school and other activities. But age alone doesn't make for maturity. Some fourteen-year-olds are much more serious about what they want to do and how they do it than a

sixteen-year-old. Interviewing and screening are especially important in junior volunteer programs.

2. Interest in a health career. It might be wise to check this with a counselor at school. A potential junior volunteer, or her mother, may insist she is interested in nursing merely to be accepted in the program.

3. Recommendations. Generally this should come from the school—a counselor, teacher or principal. It could also come from a pastor, club leader or doctor.

4. The volunteer director as well as the hospital within the community has a responsibility to the youth of the area—other than those that are just interested in health careers.

If the hospital treats alcoholics and the children are counseled by members of the hospital staff or are members of Alateens, it is well to work with these young people giving them a worthwhile job, being available when they need to talk to someone, trying to ease them of some of the confusion and conflict that is within all teen-agers who have an alcoholic parent.

5. The good volunteer director will be willing to work with juvenile officers or the local police department and help teen-agers who may be having problems in one way or another. These children, plus those mentioned in the first paragraph, are part of the community and need healing as well as hospital patients.

SELECTION

Each junior volunteer should be interviewed by the director of volunteers in somewhat the same manner as any other volunteer. The director should attempt to find out why the junior volunteer is interested. Is she genuinely interested? Is she doing it because all of her friends are signing up? Because her parents want her to do it?

The director should also find out the scope of the potential volunteer's outside activities. How involved with school and other activities is she? Is she holding a part-time job? These and similar aspects will help the director to determine how effective a volunteer the student is. Of course, a lack of outside activities can be as much of a drawback as an abundance of activities. The busiest teen-ager is often the one who gets the most done and is responsible and reliable.

Each applicant should be considered on an individual basis, but generally speaking the director should avoid the extremes.

When possible, the director should also talk to the potential volunteer's counselor or other person listed as a reference. This isn't necessary all of the time, but should be done when the director may have questions or reservations about a particular individual.

ORIENTATION AND TRAINING

A junior volunteer should receive a thorough orientation to the hospital and to the job expected of her. This should include stressing such things as ethics (gossiping about patients, etc.), conduct in the hospital, relation to patients, medical staff, employees, visitors and other volunteers and the importance of her relationship with the community as far as public relations is concerned.

A junior volunteer should also receive this material in written form. A good idea is to also have a short consent form which the parent or guardian should sign. This can be included on the application form (see appendix). From a legal point of view, this has little or no significance. However, it does let the parent know the youngster is volunteering and it also gives the parent an idea of what is expected of the junior volunteer.

It should be emphasized that orientation should be an ongoing program. As a junior volunteer becomes involved in work, the director should periodically evaluate her performance, talk to her about the work and find out if the interest in a health career is growing or declining. A common experience is that the junior volunteer is highly interested in becoming a nurse. After volunteering in the hospital, she discovers that there are many other career opportunities available in the health field. The wise director will then provide an opportunity for the young volunteer to gain experience in this area of interest.

A wise director should not be discouraged when a junior volunteer informs the director that she is no longer interested in working in the hospital. It is better for a youngster to find out now rather than when she's in college or nursing school.

Training, like orientation, should be done in the same manner as adult volunteers. Practically all things which apply to working with adult volunteers also apply to working with teen-age volunteers.

AREAS OF WORK

In the past there was a tendency to relegate junior volunteers to work in a few carefully selected and "protected" areas of the hospital. Many adult volunteer jobs are by necessity closed to the younger volunteers. Where junior volunteers work will depend upon many factors: scope of the volunteer program, types of junior volunteers, acceptance of the hospital family and similar factors.

However, here are areas in which almost all junior volunteers can work:

1. *Escort service.* Escorting patients from admitting to the patient area is a useful service.

2. *Delivery of flowers and mail.* Patients find mail and flowers even more welcome when delivered by the junior volunteers who are young and full of life.

3. *Physical therapy.* Certain types of aid work can be done here.

4. *Occupational therapy.* This is particularly good if the volunteer has an interest in crafts and manual skills.

5. *Laboratory messenger.* Delivery of specimens to the laboratories, helping with certain routine tests and general help give the future medical technologist a first-hand look at the labs.

6. *Pediatrics.* A variety of jobs can be done by the more mature junior volunteer. (Check on local and state laws on this one.)

7. *Patient aides and orderlies.* If the hospital's nursing service will provide training, younger volunteers can provide much-needed hands on a busy patient floor to provide a number of direct service needs to patients.

8. *Tray passing.* At meal time, the junior volunteer can be

FIGURE 4.   Teen-age volunteers, wearing the familiar candy stripe uniform can perform many useful jobs in the hospital while gaining valuable insights into a career in the health field.

of great assistance in helping patients get their meals promptly and even in assisting to feed some of the elderly and greatly incapacitated patients.

9. *Public contact work in the gift shop and snack shop.* Most junior volunteers enjoy this.

10. *Library cart.* Helping distribute books and magazines provides a welcome service.

This is by no means a complete list. Junior volunteers work in a wide range of capacities in numerous hospitals. The best thing for a director to do is be willing to give a junior volunteer a chance.

Just because they were never utilized in certain areas in the past, doesn't mean they can't do the job. Give it a try, have careful supervision, and the young volunteers may surprise even the most experienced director of volunteers.

BOY VOLUNTEERS

Relatively few male teen-agers have volunteered in the hospital in the past. There are numerous reasons for this, none of which are worth repeating here.

Just a few short words on the subject: treat them as men, not as girls; don't work at thinking up cute names for them; don't call them "honey," "dear" or other endearing terms.

RECOGNITION FOR TEEN-AGE VOLUNTEERS

Teen-agers seek recognition. As a part of growing up, they have a need to receive recognition for accomplishments which is why letters are given in sports, medals for musical competitions and merit badges in scouting.

A recognition program is essential for a successful junior volunteer program. A pin or a charm should be given to girl volunteers recognizing 100 hours, 250 hours and 500 hours. For more than 500 hours, a special award should be made. For boys, tie tacs may be substituted. Caps can be given to those trained as patient aides.

The volunteer group may seek to recognize outstanding young volunteers in other manners. For example, scholarships in health careers may be offered to outstanding junior volunteers.

HEALTH CAREERS

There are many methods by which health careers can be emphasized through the junior volunteer program. Here are two programs:

Condell Memorial Hospital, Libertyville, Illinois, has a health-careers educational program which seeks to provide a structured program of exposure to the various health professions to junior volunteers. Called "Penwasciz" (names for the three things

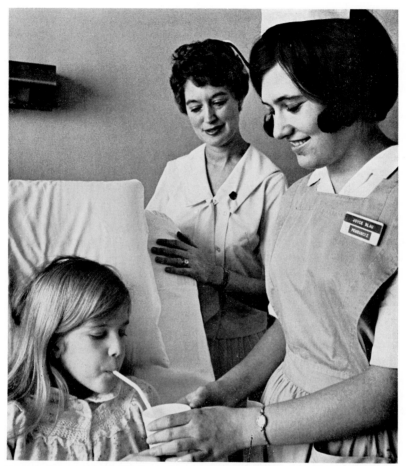

FIGURE 5. A high-school student gains valuable insight into careers in the health field in the unique "Penwasciz" at Condell Memorial Hospital, Libertyville, Illinois. (Photo courtesy of Condell Hospital.)

carried by all nurses—pen, watch and scissors) the program offers high-school boys and girls the opportunity to learn about health careers.

To participate in the program, a teen-ager must be sincerely interested in learning about health careers, must attend a two-day session for orientation and basic training, be willing to attend all scheduled meetings, assume the responsibilities for assignments and maintain a scholastic standing in school.

Participants in the program rotate from area to area to get an overall picture of the many careers available in the modern hospital. Areas include not only nursing, but dietetics, radiology, clinical laboratories, pharmacy, physical therapy, central service and other hospital departments.

Professionals from the department supervise the practical training and are available for counseling with the students. The program begins in early September and continues through the school year.

At the end of the year, a recognition program is held for those who have completed the training. A scholarship is also awarded at this time.

A program aimed at interesting young people in health careers, but in a somewhat different manner is carried on at the University of Illinois Research and Educational Hospitals, Chicago.

Elizabeth M. Morgan, R.N., coordinator of hospital volunteer services, explained the program known as C.R.E.W. (Career Related Experience Worker).

This is a cooperative program with the community agencies in which young men and women, ages sixteen to nineteen, are offered selected work experiences in the hospital setting. Although they receive a stipend from an outside agency, the hospital considers them as volunteers.

All of the young men and women are from low-income families who reside in the area adjacent to the hospital. Among the purposes of the program are to expose students to the various career opportunities in the hospital, to test the person's interest in the health field and to increase the understanding of the importance of strong academic preparation for a successful career in the health field.

Applicants were screened and interviewed by the volunteer service personnel. Orientation was also carried out through the volunteer office. Supervision on the location was provided by the supervisor in charge of the area in which the student was assigned.

Students served in eight areas of the hospital: patient floors, out-patient clinics, occupational therapy, physical therapy, surgical supply area, nursing service supply area, employee health service and the information desk.

Among the duties performed were the following:

1. Escort service.
2. Recreational program for children.
3. Assisting ward clerks on the nursing stations.
4. Preparing patients for meals.
5. Performing errands.
6. Assisting supply attendants.
7. Operating library cart.
8. Performing personal services for patients such as writing letters and similar tasks.

SUMMARY

A teen-age volunteer program in many ways is no different than an adult program. A hospital will get out of the program exactly what it puts into it.

It can be rewarding for the teen-agers or it can be frustrating and unsatisfying. With proper planning, good leadership and constant guidance, the teen-age volunteer can perform a great service to the hospital and its patients while at the same time gain valuable exposure to the multitude of career opportunities available in the modern hospital.

Leadership and direction are the critical factors.

Chapter X

WORKING WITH MALE VOLUNTEERS

H OSPITAL VOLUNTEER WORK was once the almost exclusive domain of the feminine gender. It is true that today perhaps 95 percent of hospital volunteers are female, but the number of male volunteers is showing a steady if somewhat slow growth.

True, men have provided volunteer services to hospitals for a long time. Members of the boards of trustees—an almost exclusive domain of the males—are, after all, volunteers. However, the male volunteer giving in-service is still quite rare in most hospitals.

The male volunteer probably represents the greatest potential for service. Yet, few hospitals have managed to capitalize on the wealth of talent available through male volunteers.

COMMON MISTAKES

There are numerous reasons why hospitals have not been particularly successful in gaining male volunteers.

Since hospital volunteer work has historically been work for women, most men have shunned it, not wanting to invade a woman's world. Mention hospital volunteer work to the average male and visions of pink pinafores dance in his head.

Most volunteer programs are set up for women. When a man does volunteer, the hospital usually attempts to fit him into the existing program. This may or may not work. It depends on the motivation of the man. Some are willing to volunteer any place. What works wonderfully well for women may be a total failure for men. On the other hand, a well-motivated male volunteer is perfectly willing to serve where needed.

A word of caution: if assigning a male volunteer to carry

out what had in the past been a woman volunteer's job, don't assign the man to work with women.

The types of jobs assigned and the way they are assigned are further considerations. A woman may take great delight in arranging flowers received at the reception desk. A man generally wouldn't be interested—unless, of course, he happened to be an avid gardener. He could be asked to care for plants but not to arrange flowers. His jobs should be meaningful. Masculine sounding job descriptions and orientation to the task are essential. Again, it is a matter of fitting the peg in the hole.

The demand for regular working hours plays an important role. A volunteer director thinks her best volunteers are those who can be depended upon to be at their assigned post every time. Retired male volunteers are usually very dependable. However, jobs should be scheduled so that a strict adherence to a schedule is not always essential.

Naming of the volunteers can deter men—stay away from cute titles. (There is one hospital which shall be nameless which tried to start a male volunteer program and called the volunteers the "Pink Men." The program was less than successful.)

UNIFORMS

It is necessary to have male volunteers identified in some manner. This can be done through uniforms, a blazer, a badge or a name tag. There can be some variations here, depending upon where the man is working.

A male volunteer in the business department would probably feel more comfortable in a business suit while the volunteer in a laboratory would be more at ease in a lab coat. For those working in an area such as wheel chair maintenance, it would be more practical to wear work clothes.

The idea is not necessarily uniformity, but identification that the man is a volunteer.

WHAT TO DO

A hospital or home volunteer director who is planning to utilize male volunteers should first do a great deal of research.

FIGURE 6.   Male volunteers who are handymen will often enjoy jobs such as repairing wheelchairs and similar equipment.

She should talk to agencies which are successful in using men (the YMCA for example), and talk to potential male volunteers to find what they are looking for in a program.

Age makes a great deal of difference in male volunteers—something which is not true of women volunteers. A younger man may be very involved in business so that a steady routine will just not be suitable for him. Demands of his business may make regular volunteering impossible.

On the other hand, a retired man may want to spend a lot of time at the hospital. Or, he may want to spend a lot of time at the hospital during the winter, but take off for the summer.

If there's one key word in a successful male volunteer program, it is "flexibility." A volunteer program which is flexible will have a great potential for men volunteers. A rigid program will not.

RECRUITING MEN

Most of the things which are true of recruiting women volunteers (as outlined in Chapter XI) are also true in recruiting male volunteers. However, there are some avenues open which can be used for men.

One of the best sources of male volunteers are retirees. More and more men are retiring earlier. Social security requirements limit the amount of paid work they can accept. As a result, many men are searching for meaningful work after they retire even though they can't take paid work.

Often times a hospital can capitalize on this fact. They can offer a man a job which is part pay and part volunteer.

A good time to recruit male volunteers is before retirement. Local manufacturing concerns and businesses will often supply you with names of men who are retiring. Watch the local newspapers for stories on retirement. A brief note from the volunteer director will often produce surprising results. There's no need for a hard sell here. Just say something to the effect that the hospital is always looking for interested and concerned volunteers, list a few current needs and invite the retiree to stop in and get more information.

Organized groups such as service clubs and veterans' organizations probably won't be too useful in producing volunteers. These groups are useful, however, if the hospital has need for a large group of men for a one-time effort, such as moving into a new wing, landscaping a new building or something similar. On a regular basis, however, they probably will not be very useful.

Of course, some hospitals, such as a veterans' hospital or a large mental hospital, can use a group on a regular basis. Groups can be used for different types of volunteer work including recreational therapy.

If the hospital is close to a military base, even more opportunities exist for volunteer work. However, the irregular demands of the military life coupled with frequent transfers may not result in long-term volunteers.

HOW TO GET MEN VOLUNTEERS

Pamphlets can be written up by the public relations department and circulated among the following groups: service clubs, veterans organizations and civic groups. These groups usually have committees working on health and welfare or are related to some disease problem.

List the need of volunteers of the hospital with volunteer bureaus and welfare associations if the hospital is located in a metropolitan area.

SOME GUIDELINES

1. Recognize the real motivation of male volunteer.
2. Set up a program for men.
3. Do not expect them to do such things as religiously record hours or follow a set schedule.
4. Do provide thorough training and orientation.
5. Do investigate areas thoroughly before assigning them to work.
6. Do be flexible.
7. Do provide recognition, although don't be bound by programs set up for women.
8. Do remember many retired men have been trained and have excellent experience in many fields that will benefit the hospital other than actual "In-Service" work.

HOW MALE VOLUNTEERS CAN BE USED

Male volunteers can be successfully used in many areas of the hospital. Here are some examples of imaginative use of men in volunteer positions.

1. At Presbyterian-St. Luke's Hospital of Chicago, volunteers called "stewards" visit male patients in the hospital, conducting a patient orientation. They visit patients, particularly surgical patients. Information given may range from plain reassurance to the fact that barber service is available.

2. Veterans hospitals, because they are almost exclusively male in nature, have been particularly successful in utilizing

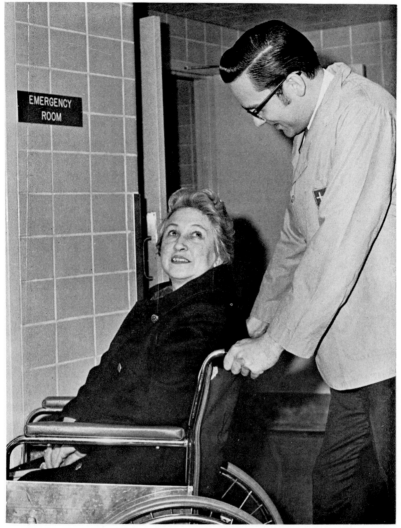

FIGURE 7. Emergency is an area where male volunteers are especially helpful in providing service.

male volunteers. For example, the VA hospital at Downey, Illinois, utilizes male volunteers on such jobs as medical illustrator, pharmacy aide, physical therapy aide, manual arts therapy aide and a multitude of other occupations.

3. The Mountainside Hospital of Glen Ridge, Montclair, New Jersey, has a Men's Volunteer Handbook containing a wel-

come, facts about the hospital, organizational chart, service requirements, hospital ethics and the volunteer pledge.

4. New York State has a Volunteer Ambulance and First Aid Association.

5. Euclid-Glenville Hospital, Euclid, Ohio, uses industry to help recruit men volunteers. The personnel directors of large local companies give printed material explaining qualifications for volunteer service, benefits of the program and a listing of the jobs available, to their employees about to retire. A definite benefit in using retired men is that they are available during the day throughout the year.

6. Good Samaritan Hospital, Santa Clara Valley, California, uses male volunteers to help during visiting hours. They are identified as male volunteers by red coats.

7. St. Paul Hospital of Dallas, Texas uses Explorer Scouts as volunteer orderlies.

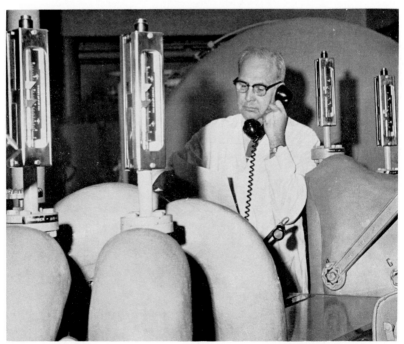

FIGURE 8.   With special training, male volunteers can often be trained for highly specialized tasks. Here a volunteer mans the controls of a hyperbaric oxygen chamber.

8. Lutheran General Hospital, Park Ridge, Illinois, utilizes male volunteers in several worthwhile projects. One retired controller assists the cost accountants prepare the financial statement for the hospital.

9. Golf Pavilion Nursing Home, Des Plaines, Illinois, uses male volunteers through various civic groups to run recreational functions for the patients.

10. The Lutheran Home for the Aged, Arlington Heights, Illinois, uses men volunteers to drive residents of the home to church and to take them shopping.

SUMMARY

The male volunteer is a somewhat recent addition to the world of volunteers. Yet, there remains a great potential for male volunteers, particularly retired men.

For a volunteer program to successfully utilize men, it is necessary for the program to be flexible. Attempting to fit a man into a program and schedule geared originally for women can result in a frustrating experience for the man and an unsuccessful program for the hospital.

But a program set up with the male in mind will produce valuable service to the hospital, and a rewarding experience for the man. This is possible if the director and staff are willing to innovate, to be flexible and to be willing to change. With an attitude like this, a successful program can be established.

Chapter XI

RECRUITING VOLUNTEERS

V ISITORS ENTERING THE hospital see volunteers in many areas. The natural assumption is that volunteers are there—they just happen. But they didn't "just happen." The volunteers were recruited.

Recruiting new members is a necessary function of all volunteer groups, large or small, new or old. New members are needed as old members die, retire, move away or lose interest. New members must also be recruited as the hospital expands its scope of services.

This chapter discusses both the philosophy of recruitment and the methods of enlisting members. The first part deals with a recruitment campaign while the second part discusses the ongoing program of gaining new members.

PHILOSOPHY OF GROUP

There are many hospital auxiliaries that are dying groups. Why? Because these groups have been made up of circles of friends who have found congenial company among themselves— so congenial that they really don't want to admit strangers to their warm little circle. As time takes its toll, these groups tend to fade away and die.

A good service organization, on the other hand, warmly welcomes new members. It, too, has warmth, but there is plenty of warmth to share with new members. As a result, the circle of volunteers grows larger and the service to the hospital increases.

Every volunteer group should regard as one of its major functions the job of making new members feel welcome and at home. The best recruitment policy an organization can have is extending friendship to each new volunteer. The organization

78

which does this will always find members ready and willing to join in service.

Recruitment will be in vain unless the new member is made to feel welcome and needed by present members of the organization. Unless the volunteer group has this feeling toward new members, it should save its time and energy in recruiting members because new members may join, but they won't stay.

SETTING UP A CAMPAIGN

There are times when it is necessary to launch a full-scale campaign to recruit volunteers. This may be in the case of a new institution which is just opening. It may be in the case of a hospital or agency which has never had a volunteer program and is now seeking volunteers. In any case, circumstances may call for a large-scale volunteer recruitment drive.

A membership drive should be carefully planned and undertaken. Here are some factors which should be taken into consideration before the first recruitment begins.

1. Why are volunteers needed? This will have to be determined before any "selling" can be done.

2. How many volunteers are needed? Getting more volunteers than needed is worse than not getting enough. There is no greater way to engender bitterness than to tell a person who has volunteered (after reading and hearing about the great need) that "Well, no, we really don't need you." Shakespeare said that "Hell hath no fury like a woman scorned" and this applies as much to a scorned volunteer as it does to a jilted lover.

3. What tools are needed? This may include advertising, film strips, brochures, speakers bureau, television spots, billboards, personal letters and news releases.

4. Who will prepare these tools? If the hospital has a public relations department, the director should be in on the planning from the start.

5. Who will use the tools when they are prepared? A great film strip may be made, but it does no good in the storage cabinet.

Careful advance planning will make a good recruitment plan successful. This presupposes that the institution has made careful plans for the utilization of volunteers once they are recruited. In addition to these steps, planning should include having these ready:

1. Application blanks.
2. Time set aside for interviewing potential volunteers.
3. A method for new volunteers to respond (a number to phone, an address to write, etc.).
4. Orientation and training sessions scheduled.
5. The readiness to put new volunteers to work as soon as possible while their enthusiasm is still high.

TOOLS OF RECRUITMENT

The types of tools to be used will vary with the type of campaign being planned. In certain cases all of these methods will be used while in some only one or two of them may be necessary. Let's look at the tools of recruitment in a bit more detail.

Personal Approach. There is no more effective method of recruiting a new member than for a volunteer to talk to another person. Nothing will succeed better.

Speakers Bureau. When attempting to reach many potential volunteers, a speakers bureau can be set up to provide programs to church groups, women's clubs, civic organizations and neighborhood clubs.

Audiovisual Aids. Perhaps the most commonly used tool here is a film strip or a 35 mm slide presentation. This can be a rather simple presentation consisting of showing a number of slides while the speaker explains them. A more elaborate presentation will have an organized group of slides with a script which the speaker can read. For a large-scale recruitment drive, a professionally done film strip with recorded narration and music can be highly effective. The thing to remember about any audiovisual presentation is this: if it's going to do any good, it's got to be used. It doesn't recruit any members if the film strip is on the closet shelf. Of course, other "audiovisuals," such as a movie could be used.

Brochures. A brochure describing the volunteer program is a highly useful tool. It is useful for utilization by an individual, when speaking to groups, as a follow-up when people write in for information and as a general "sales tool" for the volunteer organization. However, a brochure is still a tool. Its success will depend upon its usage.

News Coverage. News stories and features can be developed for local newspapers. A woman's editor can often be interested in doing a feature on a program, particularly if there is a new angle on the program—if it is expanding, adding new areas of service, et cetera.

Radio and Television Spots. Broadcast media are required to devote a certain amount of time to public service broadcasting. Some of this involves providing short announcements for civic groups. Volunteer groups can usually get time on radio and television through these public service announcements. For television, a color slide showing a volunteer in action will be useful.

Other Methods. Many other methods are available to the volunteer group. These include announcements for church bulletins, posters, billboards, mailing inserts (banks and utilities will often include an insert with their mailed statements) postage meter ads and others.

As an example of a successful recruitment campaign, Children's Hospital of Columbus, Ohio, made this report. The hospital had found that its volunteer program was growing much faster than the number of volunteers. Through a concerted recruitment drive, more than three hundred new volunteers were enrolled.

According to Willard Bailey, public relations director at Children's Hospital, a one-month drive was planned with the theme "Got time for a sick child? Volunteer at Children's Hospital."

The hospital utilized many of the methods cited above. At the conclusion of the drive, an analysis was made to determine what methods attracted the three hundred volunteers. The study showed the following breakdown:

30 percent learned about the volunteer program from newspaper stories.

26 percent from television public service announcements.

13 percent from radio announcements.

15 percent from billboards.

The remainder learned from personal visits, direct mail and other sources.

Obviously not all campaigns need to be this extensive. It may be that a volunteer director will wish to concentrate the campaign on certain groups—church women, physicians' wives, men or teenagers.

In that case, plans must be made to be able to aim directly at the groups from which recruits will be drawn. Many of the tools used in a general campaign can be used for a specific recruitment campaign. These would include brochures, speakers bureau and film strips. This type of a campaign may not include television spots, publicity campaigns or radio announcements.

ONGOING RECRUITMENT

Every volunteer group needs an ongoing program of recruitment if the organization is to stay alive and vibrant. Every volunteer has a responsibility for this, but it should also be the designated responsibility of a board member, usually a membership director. Of course, the director of volunteers is also a key person in recruitment.

Practically all of the tools used for a full-scale campaign can also be used for an ongoing program. Every volunteer group should have an informational folder available. This can be a mimeographed sheet or a multicolored printed brochure. The main thing is that it should be inviting, give full information on the volunteer program and tell the potential volunteer how to go about applying. These folders can be placed in the hospital lobby, can be distributed to new residents through the welcoming service and distributed through groups. A mention of volunteer opportunities can also be made in the patient handbook.

Volunteer recruitment is similar to advertising—constant repetition is the key to success.

ROLE OF THE MEMBERSHIP CHAIRMAN

The membership chairman should play a major role in the continuing recruitment of new volunteers. She should work closely with the director of volunteers to see that all inquiries are answered promptly, either by mail, by phone or in person, as circumstances warrant.

The membership chairman should generally be the official speaker for the volunteer organization. She should be a competent speaker who can handle herself well on the speaker's podium. She should be well versed on volunteer matters and be able to create interest and enthusiasm in her audience.

As membership chairman she should also act as an unofficial welcoming committee when new volunteers begin their service. A friendly word of welcome during that first day can be important. An invitation to have lunch in the hospital cafeteria will also be welcome. When the membership chairman can't do this in person, she should arrange for another board member or experienced volunteer to do the same thing. First impressions are lasting impressions, and if the new volunteer leaves the hospital after her first day feeling that she was warmly welcomed, she's going to turn into a faithful volunteer.

In a larger volunteer group, these duties may be split up among several workers.

ROLE OF THE DIRECTOR

The director of volunteers plays a key role in recruiting. Since she is on the job every day, she is the one who receives phone calls on volunteering. She is the one who answers the questions of people who stop in.

Even though this duty is delegated to a board membership chairman, the director of volunteers will play a key part here. She will also act as a liaison with the membership chairman, arranging for interviews, testing, orientation and training.

ROLE OF TRUSTEES

Since trustees represent the community and volunteers are members of the community, there is much in common here. Trustees can be effective aids in helping to recruit volunteers.

In order to do this, however, trustees must be informed on the full scope of volunteer services and must know that volunteers are needed. In addition, trustees also need to know the requirements for volunteer membership.

It makes the trustee look bad and creates problems for the hospital if an ill-advised trustee tells someone to "just drop by and they will put you to work." (Volunteer directors can cite similar stories from poorly informed albeit well-intended trustees, physicians, administrators and even other volunteers.)

Properly informed the trustees can be a valued ally in recruiting volunteers for the hospital. After all, trustees are volunteers themselves, and they are in a good position to sell others on the advantages of volunteering.

SOURCES OF VOLUNTEERS

Almost everyone in the community is a potential volunteer. However, certain groups will tend to produce more volunteers. As the advertisers advise "Hunt where the ducks are."

Some good sources of volunteers are as follows:

Former volunteers. Every group has a large number of former members who for various reasons no longer volunteer. Many of them stopped volunteering when home demands became greater, when they took a full-time job or similar reasons. Many times all it takes is someone asking them to return.

.Women with grown children. Women in this group now have more time available and are looking for a new challenge.

Professional career women. This is a group often overlooked by hospital volunteer organizations. A good starting point is the local Business and Professional Women's Club.

Women with young children. If they can persuade their husbands to baby sit one night a week, most welcome the chance to get out of the house. (Of course, they may prefer working in an area other than pediatrics.)

Church groups. The typical volunteer is usually an active church member. Most clergymen are glad to promote volunteer service at the hospital.

This is not meant to be an all-inclusive grouping. Rather, it shows a number of potential sources. Different communities will have different publics.

CONCLUSIONS

The best recruitment tool a volunteer group has is a satisfied volunteer. If a volunteer finds her work stimulating and satisfying, she is going to tell others about volunteering.

If the volunteer work isn't satisfying and stimulating, a hospital will have a difficult time getting and keeping volunteers. True, some people will volunteer from a sense of duty; but for a successful program, the volunteer service must be personally rewarding. If it isn't, no recruitment campaign can be successful. Perhaps a campaign can get volunteers, but it takes a good program to retain them. A good volunteer program is the best method of recruitment in the long-range program.

Chapter XII

SERVING THE COMMUNITY

$\mathbf{F}$OR MANY DECADES the University of Wisconsin has had as its unofficial motto "The boundaries of the campus are the boundaries of the state." The university recognizes that its responsibilities extend beyond the students enrolled on its campus.

It is also being recognized that the area of hospital service extends beyond the hospital walls. As a result, the volunteer organizations, made up of members of the community, are finding that their area of service is being extended to encompass the community. Those in the hospital business who crystal gaze into the future predict that the hospital of the coming years will be more and more community centered.

It is true that most hospitals are called "community" hospitals. Many hospitals have this as part of their legal name. Yet, in the past most of the concentrated effort has been placed on the patients in the hospital with little attention paid to those not in the hospital. As this attitude changes, it is realized that the area of hospital service must extend over and above the traditional clinics, free bed care and similar services provided in the past.

The volunteer group must also begin changing its traditional role to enlarge its area of service from the confines of the hospital to the borders of the community. It can work in areas which the hospital is serving and it can also show the hospital administration where it can better provide service to the community and the people there.

This means not only charitable service to medically indigent areas. It means service to all segments of the community. Since the volunteer group is made up of community members, it is in a good position to be able to provide the needed manpower, leadership and often, the financing.

86

PHILOSOPHY OF SERVICE

A volunteer group should make a self-assessment. Is it doing all it can and should be doing in the area of community health? When this question is asked, there undoubtedly will be those who will answer it by saying "There are so many things which we should be doing with the hospital which we are not doing now, how can we be expected to start giving service outside the hospital?"

Certainly no one is asking that a hospital service group abandon its in-service work. A volunteer group should strive for balance. No one asks that a hospital stop admitting patients, neither does anyone ask that a volunteer group stop providing service within the hospital.

The volunteer group should, however, when considering an expanded role of service, consider itself as part of the total hospital picture in community involvement. It should work with and as part of the hospital effort, not in an independent way.

Sometimes it may be necessary for the volunteer group to nudge the hospital and its board a bit and sometimes it may be necessary for the board and the hospital administration to nudge the volunteer group.

By working as a part of the total hospital involvement in the community, the volunteers, the hospital and the residents of the community will all be better for it. As in the case of volunteer work in the hospital, the best volunteer programs are those that are sanctioned by the trustees, backed by the administrator and given professional direction.

TYPES OF SERVICE

The type of service to the community provided by volunteers is limited only by the imagination, resources and manpower of the volunteer group. Logically, too, the needs of the particular community will help shape the type of community service. Obviously, the needs of rural Kansas, will vary considerably from those of metropolitan New York. Yet, there are needs existing in both and hospital volunteers who are working to meet these needs.

It can vary from operating a resale shop (which benefits the community and also provides income) to giving health career scholarships. It can range from aiding a research project to baby sitting with children of nurses who work in the hospital.

The types of service are endless. This chapter gives many examples. They are not all inclusive—they may not even be representative. However, they are varied and they do show some of the types of service being carried on by volunteers to help bring the hospital to the community.

Some of the services listed here are carried on at hospitals other than the hospital mentioned here. In fact, some of the programs may have even originated elsewhere and were taken up by the hospital mentioned. Certainly not every community service listed here is adaptable in each community, nor should it be. The needs of each community are separate and unique.

The community service of each volunteer group should be geared to the needs of the community and this includes community involvement. It means that the hospital and the volunteers don't tell the community: "Look, this is what you need so this is what we're going to do for you." It means listening, finding out and then beginning.

EXAMPLES OF SERVICE

Volunteers at Riverside Hospital, Toledo, Ohio, have a cooperative program with the Planned Parenthood Center to aid parents in family planning. Mrs. David G. Moore, director of volunteers, outlined the program.

In the Planned Parenthood program, a hospital trustee provided the impetus. The trustee suggested that the hospital establish a family planning clinic. The volunteer's role in the clinic is primarily educational—providing information on where planning service is available and how to obtain the assistance.

Volunteers working in the program were trained by members of the hospital's medical staff and others. Upon request of a physician, the volunteer visits a patient in the hospital and informs her of the types of planning available. The patient and the doctor make any decision on method to be used. The volunteer serves as the link between the patient and the information.

BLOOD REPLACEMENT

At Pomona Valley Community Hospital, Pomona, California, the auxiliary has for more than a decade been in charge of the blood replacement plan for the hospital. The community benefits because residents are assured of a constant supply of blood at a lower cost than if the hospital had to rely on paid donors.

According to Ernest T. Sheen, executive vice president of the hospital, the volunteers assume the responsibility for getting replacement donors. In the plan, trained volunteers visit with the patient as soon after the transfusion as possible. She explains the replacement program and tells that when he needed blood, it was available because a donor had given blood.

The volunteer explains that the replacement may be made by the patient, a family member or a friend. During the visit the volunteer tries to get a pledge for the replacement blood.

Second and third visits may be needed. Follow-up letters are used and thank you notes are mailed to those who donate blood.

Volunteers also maintain a program for maternity patients. Expectant mothers are informed that the replacement plan will provide any needed blood to the mother or child if a donation is made by a member of the family before delivery.

In a recent year, the hospital used 1,367 pints of blood. At the same time, this program helped provide 1,522 pints of blood. This means that not only are the hospital's blood needs provided for, it also means that a substantial number of pints of blood are available to the total community.

This is another example of how volunteer service can extend beyond the walls of the hospital.

CLERGY NOTIFICATION

The American Medical Association in the past years has taken an increasingly active role in the recognition that religion plays a vital role in the well-being of the hospitalization patient.

Hospitals have long recognized this, too. Trained hospital chaplains are becoming more evident in all hospitals, religious and nonsectarian as well. The local clergyman is a welcome guest at almost all hospitals.

To help facilitate the ministry of local clergymen to members of their congregations who are hospitalized, the volunteers at Mountainside Hospital in Glen Ridge-Montclair, New Jersey, have established a program to notify clergymen on the admission of patients.

Admission cards are sorted by the volunteers to eliminate patients who do not wish to have their clergymen notified or who have no church. Also, certain churches have indicated to the hospital that they do not wish to be notified. Short-term patients such as tonsil and adenoid patients are not included.

The volunteer then calls each church, informing the church that this is the hospital's chaplain office calling and that this member has been admitted to the hospital. Churches from outside the geographic area are notified by mail.

When no answer is received at the church, a second call is made the following day. If no answer is received, a card is sent to the clergyman of the patient. If the church or clergyman is new, the volunteer explains the notification program to the clergyman.

RESEARCH PROGRAMS

Not all community programs are glamorous, as one volunteer group found when it was asked to collect some 5,000 samples of sputum.

At Lutheran General Hospital, Park Ridge, Illinois, the chief pathologist and the American Cancer Society were developing a research program to see if an early method of detecting lung cancer could be developed. The study was based on the idea that cancerous cells might turn up in a person's sputum, particularly in a smoker.

Volunteers are used to collecting things: used goods for resale shops; advertisements for programs; blood for the blood bank and funds for a hospital expansion. But this was a new one.

In the program, volunteers called residents of the community, explained the program and asked for cooperation. When the resident agreed, a volunteer dropped off a sputum container at the home along with detailed instructions. The container was picked up several days later and brought to the hospital cytology laboratory.

Since the laboratory could only handle a certain number each day, the volunteers had to provide a steady number of people for the project. The research continued for several months and was judged highly successful by those directing the study.

In another research project, volunteers at Winona Community Hospital, Winona, Minnesota, provided assistance when physicians from the Communicable Disease Center of the U. S. Public Health Service visited the community to make studies on viral encephalitis in the area.

MISCELLANEOUS PROGRAMS

The Woman's Auxiliary of the Michigan State Medical Society is part of a national program to help relieve pressure on regular medical and hospital facilities. These cover such areas as homemaker service, portable meals and friendly visitors.

In the portable meals program, the group cooperates with the Mercy Hospital of Bay City, Michigan, and other health agencies to provide "mobile meals" to shut-ins. The plan provides a hot noon meal, a cold supper and supplies for the following day's breakfast. This assures the shut-in of proper nutrition. It also provides daily contact with the volunteer.

At Luther Hospital, Eau Claire, Wisconsin, members of the Service League have a "Tele-Care Program." Knowing that for people who live alone the problem of being sick and injured without anyone knowing can be a major problem.

In the "Tele-Care Program" volunteers make contact each day—usually by telephone—with people who wish to have this daily contact. Knowing that someone cares provides a great boost to many of the elderly citizens.

At Whitefish Memorial Hospital, Whitefish, Montana, volunteers assist in the annual crippled children's clinic conducted by the Montana Department of Health. Volunteers register patients, check referrals from local doctors and help with schedules.

Between 80 and 100 children are seen by visiting specialists.

At Evanston Hospital, Evanston, Illinois, volunteers were instrumental in helping the hospital set up an educational program to enable hospital employees to further their education. The volunteer group agreed to underwrite the total cost of the educational program which initially enrolled 37 employees who did not have a high school diploma.

Classes were held in the afternoon and were timed to coincide with shift changes at the hospital. Based on the first experience, the auxiliary at Evanston Hospital intends to make this an ongoing program.

At St. Barnabas Hospital, New York City, volunteers provide assistance to enable patients to vote by absentee ballot.

Some volunteers record church services and bring them to confined patients to hear.

Volunteers pick patients up and drive them to hospitals for cobalt treatment and physical therapy.

Extended care patients are assigned volunteers who follow them to their home or nursing home to visit them and do shopping for them. Some times hair appointments are taken care of by volunteers transporting patients to the beauty shop.

The Lutheran Home for the Aged in Arlington Heights, Illinois, features a shopping service for the residents of the home —toilet articles, sewing equipment and clothing. Sometimes the volunteer takes the resident with her.

Other homes for the aged have volunteers take residents to church services each Sunday at their respective churches.

EDUCATIONAL PROGRAMS

Volunteers at the Greenwich Hospital, Greenwich, Connecticut, have set up an endowment fund to provide for continuing education of hospital medical staff members and employees. Grants from the endowment can be used for anything from enabling an employee to complete high school to a postgraduate course for a medical staff member or resident.

Volunteers at St. Joseph Hospital, Kirkwood, Missouri, sponsors a scholarship program in connection with the local Meramac Junior College.

In Phoenix, Arizona, volunteers of many types help staff the

Neighborhood Doctors Office—East. It is designed to provide family doctor service to those who cannot afford private care, but do not qualify for county care.

In San Francisco, California, volunteers from Mt. Sinai Hospital and Medical Center have organized an information service. This service is designed to better inform residents of the community about the hospital's programs and facilities.

Members of the Woman's Auxiliary of the Medical Society of New Jersey cooperate in a statewide program to screen for eye defects. The program is sponsored in cooperation with hospitals, physicians and health agencies.

The eye screening program is a free public service for people over 35. It is designed to help detect evidence of any eye disease which should have treatment.

ROLE IN PUBLIC RELATIONS

Volunteers can play a major role in the total public relations program of the hospital. Since volunteers are often active members of the community, they are in a good position to be able to help interpret the institution.

The good volunteer can be an effective ambassador—if the volunteer is knowledgeable and informed about the hospital. If the volunteer is uninformed and ill informed, she is not only a poor ambassador, but she can be in a position to unwittingly harm her hospital.

The volunteer wants to be an ambassador of good will. Since she volunteers at the hospital, her friends automatically assume she's an authority on all that goes on at the institution. They ask her questions about everything from hospital costs to which gynecologist to go to.

It's true that a volunteer cannot be fully informed on every aspect of the hospital—even administrators and trustees find they can't keep up with everything. Yet, the hospital must make every effort to keep volunteers informed.

It is essential that the hospital makes the volunteer feel she is welcome, that she is needed and wanted and that she is part of the hospital family.

As pointed out by Peter N. Donatelli, administrator of

Columbia Memorial Hospital, Hudson, New York, volunteers are an effective means of reaching out to the community. He stresses that the hospital administration needs to keep volunteers fully informed if they are to be effective for the hospital.

He urges hospitals to have specialized presentations for auxiliary meetings including such people as the director of nursing, the financial director, medical directors and others.

But public relations is a two-way street. Not only should volunteers reflect the hospital to the community, but in turn the volunteers should provide feedback to the hospital from the community. This is more difficult.

First, most volunteers represent only a segment or segments of the community. Rarely are they totally representative of the community. Now there is nothing wrong with this necessarily, if this is recognized.

For example, volunteers can provide the manpower to help make an attitude survey of the community. (Examples of this are discussed in greater detail in Alvin Schwartz: *Evaluating Your Public Relations,* New York, National Public Relations Council of Health and Welfare Services, Incorporated, 1965.)

Second, there must be specific means of providing feedback. It isn't enough for an administrator to talk to a few volunteers at the awards tea and thus feel he's getting representative feedback. More than random comments are needed.

Chapter XIII

RECOGNITION FOR VOLUNTEERS

A volunteer should receive recognition for her service. True, she isn't looking for a paycheck, but she should receive some type of recognition for her contributions of time and talent. This recognition can take several forms and shapes. First, and probably most important, there has to be the inner satisfaction or recognition that she is doing something significant and worthwhile for her hospital and the people it serves.

Second, there has to be what we might term the "human recognition." Perhaps this might be a pleasant word from a hospital staff member, a friendly letter from the administrator or just a "thank you" from a patient.

Third, there should be tangible recognition. This may be a pin, a citation or another form of recognition.

Fourth, there should be some type of public recognition. This may be a picture in the paper or a public presentation of a pin.

In a large hospital, it may not be practical to have a public recognition ceremony since there might be just too many volunteers receiving awards.

One hospital, faced with this problem, has a monthly volunteer day. On this day the volunteers eligible for the service award receive their pin and are presented with a small corsage by a member of the hospital administrative staff.

Obviously no volunteer gives of her time and of herself only to receive a pin or a letter or any other such item. But it is important that this be done since it is a tangible recognition that what is being done by the volunteer is essential. It is for this reason that a good volunteer program should see that volunteers who serve faithfully are rewarded and recognized. Elementary manners dictate that a person who gives something should receive a proper "thank you," not because it is necessary, but because it is right.

Let us look at these types of recognition in more detail. If a volunteer is to get the personal satisfaction and recognition, she has to be assigned worthwhile tasks. The work she is assigned to do must be in line with her interests and talents.

The most important recognition a volunteer can have is self-recognition: the feeling that she is doing something significant and needed.

The human recognition is similar to the first point, but comes from others. This is a recognition on the part of the volunteer's co-workers in the hospital that the volunteer is giving of her time and talents.

The director of volunteers and her staff play a key role here. Although there may be hundreds of volunteers working in the hospital, the director and other staff members must try to make each individual feel needed and appreciated. If this recognition doesn't start in the volunteer service office, it probably won't be found elsewhere in the hospital.

No one, least of all the volunteer, expects a hospital staff member to fawn over her, to praise her to the sky or to keep a perpetual spotlight on her work. Yet, it is important that when a volunteer is working in contact with other members of the hospital staff that she be made to feel welcome, wanted and appreciated.

This type of recognition will do more to strengthen a volunteer's dedication than a ton of pins or a gross of certificates. The highest recognition many a volunteer wishes is the recognition that she is a vital member of the hospital team. It is a wise hospital which makes a volunteer a part of the hospital family.

The tangible recognition is quite simple, but also important. A volunteer should be given a permanent remembrance in appreciation of her service. A regular program of awards should be instituted and observed. A pin or scroll is a small token perhaps, but it is an important symbolic token and these symbols mean a great deal to the volunteer.

Finally, the public recognition. This may come through a planned program of public recognition for volunteers, through stories in hospital publications and through news stories originated by the hospital public relations department.

Incidentally, if the hospital has a public relations department, it's much wiser for the hospital to send out stories and pictures about volunteer recognition. It's just a case of it being better for someone else to say something nice about the volunteers rather than the volunteers having to say it themselves.

Depending upon the size of the community and the news media serving it, efforts should be made to have stories sent out about the awarding of service pins to volunteers. This may or may not include photos. Perhaps photos of 100-hour volunteers are quite commonplace and the photos should be saved for the volunteer for 5,000 hours. However, public recognition is important and whenever possible it should be done by the hospital itself.

Recognition also comes as a part of the hospital's ongoing public relations program. Regular mention of the volunteer program in hospital publications should be encouraged.

Care should be taken that such recognition is a part of the total hospital program. This is merely one method of noting this.

When possible, the recognition should be a hospital function; that is, the pins, certificates, or whatever, should be presented to the volunteer by a hospital representative. These should be bought and paid for by hospital funds. It enhances the prestige of the awards if they are presented by a hospital administrator or hospital trustee. These then become awards of the hospital to the volunteer and not merely the volunteers congratulating themselves on achieving certain numbers of hours.

EXAMPLES OF A PROGRAM

Each hospital will want to set its own guidelines for making awards. Many have found this system to be useful.

Bronze Pin: Awarded for 500 hours of service

Silver Pin: Awarded for 1,000 hours of service

Gold Pin: Awarded for 1,500 hours of service

A guard for the pin is awarded after 3,000 hours and a jeweled pin for 5,000 hours.

1. If the hospital is small or if not many areas are open for volunteer work, bronze pin may be given for 100 hours.
2. If more work is available, bronze pin may be given for 250 hours.
3. If hospital has a good program and there is work in many areas, bronze pin may be given for 500 hours.

Guards may be given for added hours (1) from 100 hours (2) 250 hours to (3) 500 hours.

TYPES OF AWARDS

The small volunteer group will probably find it more convenient to use a stock award pin such as those available through the American Hospital Association. These are attractive, are available in classifications ranging from 100 hours to 10,000 hours and are quite reasonable when a small number of pins are required.

The larger volunteer group which may require several dozen or more pins each year will probably prefer to have a custom designed pin made, incorporating the seal of the hospital or the insignia of the volunteer group. There are a number of firms which specialize in this service.

SPECIAL AWARDS

A volunteer group will probably also wish to set up special awards. This may include an award to the outgoing president and board members. It may also be to a special volunteer who has done certain types of work or has worked for a certain number of years which somehow seems to fit outside a regular category.

However, a group would be wise to be extremely sparing of special awards. If a special award becomes commonplace, it is no longer a "special" award.

SPECIAL EVENTS

When possible, service awards should be presented at a public event. This can take many forms ranging from a regular meeting to a fashionable tea or luncheon. The type of event will depend a great deal upon the hospital and the volunteers.

When possible, the event should be officially hosted by the hospital's board or administration or both. Of course, volunteers know from a practical point they may end up doing the work anyway, but the board or administration should issue the invitations and pick up the check.

There is no need to have every award function be identical to the last one. The wise volunteer group will offer variety. From time to time it might be a good idea to invite the spouses or families.

In smaller communities, the old fashioned potluck dinner may be a workable idea.

OTHER MEANS OF RECOGNITION

1. Recognize the volunteer by the gift of free meals each time they work.

2. Promote the volunteer to a volunteer job having more responsibility.

3. Elect them to a board position.

Chapter XIV

VOLUNTEER ROLE IN FUND RAISING

In 1968, HOSPITALS in the United States received gifts totaling an estimated $1,400,000,000. While no figures are available, it is the feeling of most knowledgeable fund raisers that the greatest single source of hospital funds comes through auxiliaries and volunteer groups.

In fact, many hospitals owe their origin to the efforts of groups of volunteer women. Hospital history after history begin with the words "The history of this hospital began when a small group of women raised funds to purchase a small frame house for use as a hospital." These histories recount the many methods which the volunteer used to provide funds for the struggling medical institutions.

The funds raised by volunteers are important to the hospital. Many a hospital building drive has been guided to success by the diligent work of the volunteers. Countless pieces of equipment, many educational programs and innumerable charitable clinics would not be a reality without the fund raising of these volunteers.

At the same time, a great change has occurred. The typical hospital auxiliary in years gone by was organized primarily for fund raising purposes. This is true today of many hospital auxiliaries.

With groups set up to provide volunteer service, fund raising represents an important function. Yet, it is important to remember that fund raising should be a by-product of service rather than the principal aim of the volunteers. Volunteers should be in the hospital to provide service, and some of this service will result in funds being raised.

A volunteer organization which is devoted exclusively to

fund raising may ultimately be doing a disservice to the hospital it is seeking to serve.

PHILOSOPHY OF FUND RAISING

Fund raising by volunteers—like Caesar's wife—should be above reproach. The American Hospital Association, in action approved in 1964, sets these guidelines for fund raising by volunteer groups.

1. Fund raising should be a by-product of service.
2. Fund raising should be used as a vehicle for telling the hospital's story to the community.
3. Fund raising could also be a part of a hospital-initiated and directed capital fund drive.

If these three general guidelines are kept in mind, fund raising by volunteers will be kept in the proper perspective within the group and within the hospital.

The auxiliary should remember that the bulk of the community will equate the activities of the volunteer group with the hospital itself. Cheap methods of fund raising will tend to lower the public esteem of the hospital.

No volunteer would, hopefully, do anything which would injure the reputation of her hospital. Yet, the same volunteer will jeopardize the reputation of the hospital by less than ethical fund raising, justifying it on the basis of "Well, after all it is for a good cause" or "Well, everyone else does it too."

If the law of the community says no raffles, the auxiliary should not hold a raffle even though it can get away with it. If the law of the community says slot machines are illegal, don't have them at the picnic.

TYPES OF FUND RAISING

Let us look at service type of fund raising in more detail.

Fund raising should have a dual purpose: service and funds. And the purposes should be in that order. Here are some examples of how volunteers can carry out this twofold philosophy.

Gift Shop. Gift shops are among the most common forms of

FIGURE 9.   A gift shop run by volunteers can be of service to patients and visitors while at the same time providing needed funds for the hospital.

service and fund raising projects. They are generally located in the hospital lobby and can range from a display cabinet with a few gifts to a full-scale store with paid employees in addition to volunteer help. Regardless of size, the gift shop should provide service. It should stock items needed by hospital patients, as well as items which add to the comfort and well being of patients. In addition, it should also provide items which are of service to hospital staff members and visitors. Items should be priced fairly.

Snack Shop. Many hospitals, particularly newer ones, are located away from commercial eating establishments. As a result, patient visitors appreciate a spot where they can get a cup of coffee or a snack. A snack shop is an excellent service, appreciated by visitors and staff alike.

Resale Shops. A resale shop, thrift shop or second-hand store is another excellent service opportunity for hospital volunteer groups. These are usually located outside the hospital and sell good used merchandise, donated by members and others, at a reasonable cost to people in the community.

Television Rental. Third-party payers of hospital care are raising questions as to whether television should be a part of the hospital charges. As a result, more and more hospitals are making television an optional item. Television sets can be rented as a convenience to hospital patients who wish to have the sets.

Baby Photos. Most parents appreciate having a photo of their new baby taken shortly after birth.

Memorial Fund. Many people today prefer to make a gift to a hospital or other agency as a memorial to a departed friend or relative. The volunteer group is a natural organization to handle this type of a program.

Benefits. It is hard to say which came first in a hospital auxiliary—the formal organization or the sponsorship of the first benefit. Benefits and luncheons and dinner dances are very much a part of the American volunteer scene. There has been a tendency in recent years for these benefits to become less formal than in past years.

Christmas Cards. A good method of raising funds is for the volunteer groups to provide Christmas cards in return for donations.

These types of fund raising are good because they are continuous, providing a constant flow of money for the hospital. In addition, volunteers who for one reason or another do not want to work in direct contact with patients can be effectively utilized here.

A POTENTIAL TROUBLE SPOT

For the service-minded volunteer group, fund raising becomes a potential trouble spot. It becomes a potential downfall of the organization if the organization fails to keep in mind that money is a by-product of the organization, not its main purpose for being in existence.

It is easy to see why this can happen. Most hospitals are short of funds and have more needs than there are funds available. As a result, the funds raised by volunteer groups are highly important. Many a hospital expansion and many a hospital piece of equipment would not be available if it were not for the funds provided by the volunteer group.

Because of this, there is a temptation on the part of administration and trustees to begin asking the volunteers for more funds for this project and that project. As a result, the volunteers may begin viewing their monetary contribution as being more important than their contribution of time and talents.

It's easy to understand why this can happen. Money is tangible—service is intangible. A trustee can see a contribution of money. He cannot see a contribution of service.

PROPER BALANCE NEEDED

It is a wise board and a wise administration which recognizes and constantly stresses that services provided by volunteers are much more important than the money. When the fund raising part of the volunteer group is kept in its proper perspective, then the volunteers are truly making a significant contribution to the hospital and its program. Perhaps it is somewhat difficult to know where a proper balance may lie. Here are some ways a volunteer group can test itself on whether or not it is devoting too much time and effort to fund raising:

1. At the next volunteers board meeting make note of how much board time is spent on items such as benefits, finances, and related topics compared with the amount of time spent on such items as new areas of service, recruiting volunteers and similar aspects.

2. Take a ruler and the last several copies of the volunteers newsletter. Measure how much space discusses service projects and how much discusses fund raising projects.

3. Take a look at the last dozen news releases sent out about the volunteers. How many discuss service and how many discuss money?

4. Check the trustee minutes in reference to volunteers. How much time is spent on fund raising aspects and how much time is spent on service aspects?

These are not all-inclusive, but a little self-examination by the volunteers may be worthwhile. Perhaps the examination should also come from the trustees or hospital administration. This is not meant to downgrade the very substantial financial contributions made to the nation's hospitals by volunteers. But in the long run, the volunteer group which provides service as its main contribution, with money as a secondary consideration, will find that it is making a much greater contribution to the hospital and to the people the hospital serves. Equally important, the members of the volunteer group will receive much greater satisfaction because they know they are giving of themselves.

As discussed earlier in this chapter, projects such as a resale shop, a gift shop, baby photos and similar items are excellent projects because they not only raise funds but they also provide a needed service at the same time.

SUMMARY

In summary, it should be pointed out that there is something unique about each hospital. For the hospital volunteer group which has historically regarded itself as primarily a fund-raising organization, there is no need to suddenly stop all fund-raising activities. To do so might be a disaster for the hospital if the hospital depends upon these funds to conduct its educational programs or charitable work.

Yet, it is the responsibility of the hospital—trustees, administrators and volunteers—to examine itself and attempt to determine what the role of the volunteer should be.

Just as the role of the modern hospital is changing, so is the role of its volunteers. The volunteer group which is operating as it did twenty-five, ten or even five years ago is probably now outdated just as the hospital which does not keep up with the times becomes outdated.

The volunteer group must keep pace with changes in the hospital field. Not to do so would make the volunteers derelict in their duty to the hospital, patients and community.

BIBLIOGRAPHY

BOOKS

1. *Art of Christian Relationships*, Student's Resource Book. Minneapolis, Minn., Augsburg Publishing House, 1967. This book helps the individual learn the art of Christian relationships to the improvement of all life's relationships and also teaches how to participate in group life.
2. Church, David M.: *How to Succeed with Volunteers*. New York, National Public Relations Council of Health and Welfare Services, Inc., 1963. One of the many excellent books published by this organization. This is well worth reading for the volunteer leader.
3. *Citizen Volunteer*. Cohen, Nathan E.: New York, Harper & Brothers, 1960. This book gives a clear picture of the history of the volunteer in the growth of America and explains the importance of volunteerism as related to democracy and covers questions of individual motivation: Why should I help? What can I do? What does it mean to me? It describes various volunteer fields and gives good ideas on recruitment and utilization of citizen volunteers.
4. Duff, Raymond S., and Hillingshead, August B.: *Sickness and Society*. New York, Harper & Row, 1968. This book explores interrelationships between patient and family, the hospital, doctors and hospital personnel and tells of the influences of physical disease as well as those of home, community and hospital social systems; and relates these influences and their impact upon patient care and the patient.
5. Hayt, Jonathan: *Law for Hospital Auxiliaries*. Albany, N. Y., Hospital Educational and Research Fund in collaboration with Hospital Association of New York State, 1964. *Law for Hospital Auxiliaries* is a must for volunteer directors and auxiliary presidents to read.
6. Houle, Cyril O.: *The Effective Board*. New York, Association Press, 1962. This is a good reference for working with a voluntary board.
7. Kurtz, Harold P.: *Public Relations for Hospitals*. A Practical Handbook. Springfield, Ill., Charles C Thomas, 1969. It is an excellent reference book for all volunteer directors. It gives good guide lines on working with photographers, cooperating with news media and many day to day activities that are related to volunteer work and community relations, as well as hospital public relations.

8. Lambourne, R. A.: *Community, Church and Healing.* London, Darton, Longman & Todd, 1963. Since volunteers are of the community and usually have a church background, this book gives valuable insight on the relationship of healing, the community and the church along with some unusual observations and conclusions.
9. Lehrer, Robert N.: *Work Simplification.* Englewood Cliffs, N. J., Prentice-Hall, Inc. Because a director of volunteers does not always have a business background, or has not managed an office of any kind, this book would be most helpful. Examples are cited to show how to solve typical work problems, etc. Dr. Lehrer also explains the importance of the human factor in work simplification.
10. Lockerby, Florence K.: *Communication for Nurses.* Third edition. St. Louis, The C. V. Mosby Company, 1968. Although this book is written for nurses, the information it imparts on communications is useful for anyone to read whose job deals with people.
11. Scharlemann, Martin H.: *Healing and Redemption.* St. Louis, Concordia Pub. House, 1965. This is written for doctors, nurses, missionaries and pastors on human wholeness and is good for anyone working with ill people.
12. *The Volunteer in the Hospital.* Chicago, American Hospital Association, 1959. It is valuable to any volunteer director's library and gives guide lines to organizing and developing volunteer programs in large or small hospitals.
13. Wilson, Michael: *The Church is Healing.* Naperville, Ill., SCM Book Club, 1966. This describes the church's ministry of healing and our ministry to those who suffer. It helps hospital workers to more fully understand "illness" and what is meant by "wholeness."

PAMPHLETS, FOLDERS AND CATALOGS

American Hospital Association: *Catalog of Visual Aids.* This lists audio-visual material that can be used for the volunteer department.
American Hospital Association: *Guidelines for Auxiliary Fund Raising.* Guidelines for fund raising activities.

PERIODICALS

American Hospital Association: *Hospitals J.A.H.A.* This provides annual review of volunteer services, frequent news on new volunteer ideas and occasional articles on the subject.
American Hospital Association: *The Volunteer Leader.* The only magazine published exclusively on the subject of hospital volunteers.

McGraw-Hill Publishing Co.: *Modern Hospitals*. Contains regular material on the subject.

American Hospital Association: *Public Relations Newsletter*. This monthly four-page bulletin contains some ideas on volunteers and hospitals.

National Public Relations Council of Health and Welfare Inc.: *Channels*. This semi-monthly bulletin is invaluable for the volunteer leader in the not-for-profit field.

JOB DESCRIPTION FOR THE DIRECTOR OF HOSPITAL VOLUNTEERS

THE FOLLOWING JOB description for the director of hospital volunteers, approved by the American Hospital Association's Board of Trustees, is intended to serve only as a guide to hospitals in selecting their directors of volunteers. In the final analysis, the individual hospital must establish its own qualifications for the person who will hold the job of director of volunteers in the hospital.

Main Function: Assists administrators and departmental directors in obtaining and retaining an adequate, competent and satisfied volunteer staff, and provides certain centralized volunteer service.

Responsible to: Administrator or assistant administrator.

Duties and Responsibilities: Formulates and recommends to administration volunteer policies, standards, programs, and means for their administration; conducts necessary studies for the dynamic development of the department; keeps informed on legal regulations; maintains contacts with administration and departmental directors to learn of hospital needs and problems; generally assists in maintaining volunteer morale.

Interprets volunteer policy, notifies administration and department heads of volunteer departmental policy decisions, and maintains, for using departments, written guides on volunteer policies and procedures.

Develops and maintains a sound volunteer organizational structure.

Assists administration and departmental directors in establishing volunteer jobs and attaining maximum utilization of volunteer personnel.

Develops a program of recruitment, induction, and orientation of volunteers; screens and refers for placement. Develops, with the personnel director, a program of employee orientation to the volunteer program.

Assists administration and department heads by developing the following:

> Methods and procedures for periodic appraisal of volunteer performance; training; communications; promotion to other volunteer jobs; handling dissatisfaction; disciplinary actions, and exit interviews.
>
> Policies relating to work hours (schedules, limitations) and to sick leave, vacation, holidays, and other leaves of absence.
>
> A program of job descriptions, evaluation, and recognition for volunteers.
>
> Policies for benefits which may be made available by the hospital, such as free meals for volunteers.

Plans, develops and supervises maintenance of volunteer records, statistics and reports; prepares departmental budget.

Participates as requested in hospital programs, such as fire drills, safety campaigns, disaster preparedness and community chest drives.

As required by hospital, oversees the preparation and filing of accident reports for workmen's compensation and other insurance; reviews the on-job accident experience record of volunteers.

Develops and maintains a program of liaison with the hospital auxiliary as approved by administration.

Maintains contact with department heads; volunteers and employees of all departments; volunteer applicants; and various community agencies.

Education: Bachelor's degree (suggested major in the behavioral sciences).

Experience: Not less than two years' executive or administrative experience.

Personal Qualifications: The director of volunteers must be able to meet the special demands made on him as a result of the extraordinary amount of interpersonal and interdepartmental relationships involved in the position.

The director of volunteers requires a different leadership

quality for direction and supervision of nonpaid workers than for direction of paid employees.

The director of volunteers must be able to carry a high degree of responsibility for the hospital's community relations, since the volunteer is of and from the community.

The director of volunteers must be able to perform comfortably in working relationships with volunteers who represent a broad spectrum of educational achievement and different elements in the community.

(Reprinted through the courtesy of the American Hospital Association.)

Appendix 2

ETHICS FOR VOLUNTEERS

1. Loyalty to the hospital is essential.
2. Volunteers should regard as confidential everything seen or heard in the hospital. All matters pertaining to patients, physicians and personnel are confidential and should be regarded as such at all times, both in the hospital and in the community. Failure to do this is just cause for dismissal of a volunteer.
3. Have a professional attitude in all contacts and maintain the standards of the hospital at all times.
4. Volunteers are directly responsible to the person in charge of the department or area in which they are working.
5. Never ask a patient the reason he is in the hospital. Never discuss your own hospital experiences with a patient. Never, under any circumstances, attempt to give advice or render an opinion as to diagnosis or treatment as this might be interpreted as coming from medical authority. Only physicians are legally authorized to give medical advice and opinions.
6. Whenever there appears to be a cause for criticism, please bring the matter to the attention of the director of volunteers.
7. Speak softly in a pleasant, modulated voice.
8. Do not smoke or chew gum while on duty.
9. Do not wear earrings, bracelets or necklaces.
10. While on duty volunteers must wear clean, neatly pressed uniforms. Shoes must be low-heeled, preferably white.

Appendix 3

VOLUNTEER'S PLEDGE

BELIEVING THAT THE hospital has real need of my service as a volunteer worker,

I will be punctual and conscientious in the fulfillment of my duties and accept supervision graciously.

I will conduct myself with dignity, courtesy and consideration.

I will consider as confidential all information which I hear directly or indirectly concerning a patient, doctor or any member of the personnel and will not seek information in regard to a patient.

I will take any problems, criticisms or suggestions to the Director of Volunteers. I will endeavor to make my work of the highest quality.

I will uphold the traditions and standards of this hospital, and will interpret them to the community at large.

Appendix 4

PRAYER FOR VOLUNTEERS

ALMIGHTY GOD AND Heavenly Father of Mankind, bless we pray Thee, our endeavors in those hospitals in which we strive to bring comfort and hope to all who are in distress of mind or body.

Guide us so that we may use the privilege given us to help the aged, the ill and the very young—with generosity, with discretion and with gentleness.

Give us the strength to labor diligently, the courage to think and to speak with clarity and conviction, but without prejudice or pride.

Grant us, we beseech Thee, both wisdom and humility in directing our united efforts to do for others only as Thou would have us do. Amen.

SAMPLE: TEEN-AGE VOLUNTEER APPLICATION

Name _____

          Last   First

Address _____Home Telephone _____

Town _____

Name of High School _____School Year _____

Date of Birth _____

Parents Name _____Phone _____

Address _____Town _____

Parents Consent, Signature _____

Referred by _____

Church, Clubs—other organizations _____

_____

Scheduled Responsibilities _____

Summer School, Baby Sitting, etc. _____

Which of the following Health Careers are you planning:

Doctor	Social Work
Nurse	Dietitian
Physical Therapy	Medical Records
Occupational Therapy	Laboratory Technologist
Recreational Therapy	X-Ray Technician
Pharmacy	Other _____

Appendix 6

TO BE FILLED OUT BY DEAN
OR COUNSELOR

What Health Field is student interested in?
How serious is student about this career?
What courses is student now taking in preparation for this career?
Status as to grades.
Any other comments.

Signature _____

Title _____

Date _____

Please have Dean or Counselor return this application.

INDEX